Francis Marion Crawford

A Rose of Yesterday

Francis Marion Crawford

A Rose of Yesterday

ISBN/EAN: 9783744685283

Printed in Europe, USA, Canada, Australia, Japan

Cover: Foto ©Thomas Meinert / pixelio.de

More available books at **www.hansebooks.com**

A ROSE OF YESTERDAY

BY

F. MARION CRAWFORD

AUTHOR OF "SARACINESCA," "DR. CLAUDIUS," "KATHARINE LAUDERDALE," "THE RALSTONS," ETC., ETC.

New York
THE MACMILLAN COMPANY
LONDON: MACMILLAN & CO., LTD.
1897

All rights reserved

Copyright, 1897,
By F. MARION CRAWFORD.

A ROSE OF YESTERDAY

CHAPTER I

"I WONDER what he meant by it," said Sylvia, turning again in her chair, so that the summer light, softened and tinted by the drawn blinds, might fall upon the etching she held.

"My dear," answered Colonel Wimpole, stretching out his still graceful legs, leaning back in his chair, and slowly joining his nervous but handsome hands, "nobody knows."

He did not move again for some time, and his ward continued to scrutinize Dürer's Knight. It was the one known as 'The Knight, Death, and the Devil,' and she had just received it from her guardian as a birthday present.

"But people must have thought a great deal about it," said Sylvia, at last. "There must be stories about what it means. Do tell me. I'm sure you know."

She laid the unframed print upon her knees, still holding it by the edges, lest the fitful breeze that came in through the blinds should blow it to the floor. At the same time she raised her eyes till they met the colonel's.

Her earnest young face expressed something like veneration as she gazed at him, and perhaps he thought that it was undeserved, for he soon looked away, with a faint sigh. She sighed, too, but more audibly, as though she were not ashamed of it. Possibly she knew that he could not guess what the sigh meant, and the knowledge added a little pain to what she felt just then, and had felt daily of late. She began to study the etching again.

"To me," she said softly, "the Knight is a hero. He is making Death show him the way, and he has made the Devil his squire and servant. He will reach the city on the hill in time, for there is still sand enough in the hour-glass. Do you see?" She held out the print to the colonel. "There is still sand enough," she repeated. "Don't you think so?"

Again, as she asked the question, she looked at him; but he was bending over the etching, and she could only see his clear profile against the shadows of the room.

"He may be just in time," he answered quietly.

"I wonder which house they lived in, of those one can see," said Sylvia.

"Who are 'they'? Death, the Devil, and the Knight?"

"No. The Knight and the lady, of course,—the lady who is waiting to see whether he will come in time."

The colonel laughed a little at her fancy, and looked at her as the breeze stirred her brown hair. He did not understand her, and she knew that he did not. His glance took in her brown hair, her violet eyes, her delicately shaded cheek, and the fresh young mouth with its strange little half-weary smile that should not have been there, and that left the weariness behind whenever it faded for a time. He wondered what was the matter with the girl.

She was not ill. That was clear enough, for they had travelled far, and Sylvia had never once seemed tired. The colonel and Miss Wimpole, his elderly maiden sister, had taken Sylvia out to Japan to meet her father, Admiral Strahan, who had been stationed some time with a small squadron in the waters of the far East. He had been ordered home rather suddenly, and the Wimpoles were bringing the girl back by way of Europe. Sylvia's mother had been dead three years, and had left her a little fortune. Mrs. Strahan had been a step-sister, and no blood relation, of the Wimpoles; but they had been as a real brother and a real sister to her, and she had left her only child to their care during such times as her husband's service should keep him away from home. The girl was now just eighteen.

Colonel Wimpole wondered whether she could be destined for suffering, as some women are, and the thought linked itself to the chain of another life, and drew it out of his heart that he might see it and be hurt, for he had known pain in himself and through one he loved. He could not believe that Sylvia was forefated to sorrow, and the silent weariness that of late was always in her face meant something which he feared to learn, but for which he felt himself vaguely responsible, as though he were not doing his duty by her.

He was a man of heart, of honour, and of conscience. Long ago, in his early youth, he had fought bravely in a long and cruel war, and had remained a soldier for many years afterwards, with an old-fashioned attachment for arms that was dashed with chivalry, till at last he had hung up his sword, accepting peace as a profession. Indeed he had never loved anything of war, except its danger and its honour; and he had loved one woman more than either, but not against honour nor in danger, though without any hope.

He had lived simply, as some men can and

as a few do live, in the midst of the modern world, parting with an illusion now and then, and fostering some new taste in its place, in a sort of innocent and simple consciousness that it was artificial, but in the certainty that it was harmless. He was gentle in his ways, with the quiet and unaffected feeling for other people which not seldom softens those who have fought with their hands in the conviction of right, and have dealt and received real wounds. War either brutalizes or refines a man; it never leaves him unchanged. Colonel Wimpole had travelled from time to time, more for the sake of going to some one place which he wished to see, than of passing through many places for the sake of travelling. There is a great difference between the two methods. Wherever he went, he took with him his own character and his slightly formal courtesy of manner, not leaving himself at home, as some people do, nor assuming a separate personality for Europe, like a disguise; for, such as he was, he was incapable of affectation, and he was sure that the manners which had been good enough for his mother were good enough for any woman in the world, as indeed they were, because he was a gentleman, that is, a man, and gentle at all points, excepting for his honour. But no one had ever touched that.

He looked what he was, too, from head to foot. He was a tall, slender man, of nervous strength, with steady grey eyes, high features, smooth, short and grizzled hair; simple and yet very scrupulous in his dress; easy in his movements; not old before his time, but having already something of the refinement of age upon the nobility of his advanced manhood; one of whom a woman would expect great things in an extremity, but to whom she would no longer turn for the little service, the little fetching and carrying, which most women expect of men still in prime. But he did such things unasked, and for any woman, when it seemed natural to do them. After all, he was only fifty-three years old, and it seems to be established that sixty is the age of man's manumission from servitude, unless the period of slavery be voluntarily extended by the individual. That leaves ten years of freedom if one live to the traditional age of mankind.

But Sylvia saw no sign of age in Colonel Wimpole. In connexion with him the mere word irritated her when he used it, which he sometimes did quite naturally, and he would have been very much surprised could he have guessed how she thought of him, and what she was thinking as she sat looking from him to Dürer's Knight and from the etched rider to the living man again. For she saw a resemblance which by no means existed, except, perhaps, between two ideals.

The Knight in the picture is stern and strong and grim, and sits his horse like the incarnation of an unchanging will, riding a bridled destiny against Death and Evil to a good end. And Death's tired jade droops its white head and sniffs at the skull in the way, but the Knight's charger turns up his lip and shows his teeth at the carrion thing and arches his strong neck, while the Knight looks straight before him, and cares not, and his steel-clad legs press the great horse into the way, and his steel-gloved hand holds curb and snaffle in a vise. As for the Devil, he slinks behind, an evil beast, but subdued, and following meanly with a sort of mute, animal astonishment in his wide eyes.

And beside Sylvia sat the colonel, quiet, gentle, restful, suggesting just then nothing of desperate determination, and not at all like the grim Knight in feature. Yet the girl felt a kinship between the two, and saw one and the same heroism in the man and in the pictured rider. In her inmost heart she wished that she could have seen the colonel long ago, when he had fought, riding at death without fear. But the thought that it had been so very long ago kept the wish down, below the word-line in her heart's well. Youth clothes its ideals with the spirit of truth and hides the letter out of sight.

But in the picture, Sylvia looked for herself, since it was for a lady that the Knight was riding, and all she could find was the big old house up in the town, on the left of the tallest tower. She was waiting somewhere under the high-gabled roof, with her spinning-wheel or her fine needlework, among her women. Would he ever come? Was there time before the sand in Death's hour-glass should run out?

"I wish the horse would put his fore foot down, and go on!" she said suddenly.

Then she laughed, though a little wearily. How could she tell the colonel that he was the Knight, and that she was waiting in the tall house with the many windows? Perhaps he was never to know, and forever the charger's fore foot would be lifted, ready for the step that was never to fall upon the path.

But Colonel Wimpole did not understand. It was unlike her to wish that an old print should turn into a page from a child's movable picture-book.

"Why do you wish that the horse would go on?" he asked half idly.

"Because the sand will not last, if he waits," said Sylvia, quietly; and as she spoke a third time of the sand in the hour-glass, she felt a little chill at her heart.

"There will always be time," answered the colonel, enigmatically.

"As there will always be air, I suppose; and that will not matter to us, when we are not here to breathe it any more."

"That is true. Nothing will matter very much a hundred years hence."

"But a few years matter much more than a hundred." Her voice was sad.

"What are you thinking of?" asked Colonel Wimpole, changing his position so as to see her face better.

He resented her sadness a little, for he and his sister were doing their best to make her happy. But Sylvia did not answer him. She bent her white forehead to the faint breeze that came through the closed green blinds, and she looked at the etching. The colonel believed that she was thinking of her dead mother, whom she had loved. He hesitated, choosing his words, for he hated preaching, and yet it seemed to him that Sylvia mourned too long.

"I was very fond of your mother, too, my dear," he said gently, after a time. "She was like a real sister to us. I wish I could have gone instead, and left her to you."

"You?" Sylvia's voice startled him; she

was suddenly pale, and the old print shook in her hands. "Oh, no!" she cried half passionately. "Not you—not you!"

The colonel was surprised for a moment. Then he was grateful, for he felt that she was very fond of him. He thought of the woman he loved, and that he might have had such a daughter as Sylvia, but with other eyes.

"I am glad you are fond of me," he said. "You are very good to me, and I know I am a tiresome old man."

At that word, one beat of the girl's heart sent resentful blood to her face.

"You are not old at all!" she cried. "And you could not be tiresome if you tried! And I am not good to you, as you call it!"

The girl's young anger made him think of summer lightning, and of the sudden flashing of new steel drawn silently and swiftly from the sheath into the sunshine.

"Goodness may be a matter of opinion, my dear," said he. "But age is a matter of fact. I was fifty-three years old on my last birthday."

"Oh, what do years matter?" Sylvia rose quickly and turned from him, going towards the window.

The colonel watched her perfectly graceful

movements. She wore grey, with a small black band at her throat, and the soft light clung to the lovely outline of her figure and to her brown hair. He thought again of the daughter that might have been born to him, and even of a daughter's daughter. It seemed to him that his own years might be a greater matter than Sylvia would admit. Yet, as their descending mists veiled hope's height, he was often glad that there should not be as many more as there had been. He said nothing, and there was a dream in his eyes.

"You are always saying that you are old. Why?" Sylvia's voice came from the window, but she did not turn. "It is not kind," she said, still more softly.

"Not kind?" He did not understand.

"It is not kind to me. It is as though I did not care. Besides, it is not true!"

Just then the conviction had come back to her voice, stronger than ever, strengthening the tone just when it was breaking. She had never spoken to him in this way. He called her.

"Sylvia! Will you come here, my dear?" She came, and he took her fresh young hands. "What is it? Has anything happened? Are you unhappy? Tell me."

At his question the violet eyes slowly filled,

and she just bent her head once or twice, as though assenting.

"You are unhappy?" He repeated his question, and again she nodded sadly.

"But happy, too, — often."

There was not room for happiness and sorrow together in her full eyes. The tear fell, and gladness took its place at his touch. But he looked, and remembered other hands, and began to know the truth. Love's unforgotten spirit came, wafting a breath of older days.

He looked, and wondered whom the girl had chosen, and was glad for her happiness while he grew anxious for its life. She was so young that she must have chosen lately and quickly. In a rush of inward questioning his mind ran back through the long journey they had made together, and answers came in many faces of men that glided before him. One of them stopped him and held his thought, as a fleeting memory will. A young officer of her father's flagship, lean, brown, bright-eyed, with a strong mouth and a rare smile. Sylvia had often talked with him, and the boy's bright eyes used to watch her from the distance when he was not beside her. Quiet of speech he was, and resolute, bred in the keen air of a northern sea, of the few from among whom fate may choose the one. That was the man.

The colonel spoke, then, as though he had said much, glad and willing to take the girl's conclusion.

"I know who it is," he said, as if all had been explained. "I am glad, very glad."

His hands pressed hers more tightly, for he was a man of heart, and because his own life had failed strangely, he knew how happy she must be, having all he had not. But the violet eyes grew wide and dark and surprised, and the faint colour came and went.

"Do you really, really know at last?" she asked, very low.

"Yes, dear, I know," he said, for he had the sure conviction out of his sympathy for the child.

"And you are glad? Even as I am?"

"Indeed I am! I love you with all my heart, my dear."

She looked at him a moment longer, and then her sight grew faint, and her face hid itself against his coat.

"Say it! Say it again!" she repeated, and her white fingers closed tightly upon his sleeve. "I have waited so long to hear you say it!"

An uneasy and half-distressed look came to his face instantly, as he looked down at the brown hair.

"What?" he asked. "What have you waited to hear me say?"

"That — the words you said just now." Her face still hidden, she hesitated.

"What did I say? That I loved you, my dear?"

She nodded silently, against his coat.

"That I have always loved you, Sylvia dear," he said, while a wondering fear stole through him.

"You never told me. And I did not dare tell you — how could I? But now you understand. You know that the years mean nothing, after all, and that there is still sand in the hourglass, and you and I shall reach the end of the road together —"

"Sylvia!" His voice rang sharply and painfully as he interrupted her.

He was a little pale, and his grey eyes were less steady than usual, for he could not be mistaken any longer. He had faced many dangers bravely, but the girl frightened him, clinging to his sleeve, and talking of her half-childish love for him. Then came the shock to his honour, for it seemed as though it must somehow have been his fault.

She looked up and saw his face, but could not understand it, though she had a prevision of evil, and the stealing sickness of disappointment made her faint.

"I did not know what you meant, my child,"

he said, growing more pale, and very gently pushing her back a little. "I was thinking of young Knox. I thought you loved him. I was so sure that he was the man."

She drew back, now, of her own will, staring.

"Knox? Mr. Knox?" She repeated the name, hardly hearing her own words, half stunned by her mistake. "But you said — you said you loved me —"

"As your father does," said Colonel Wimpole, very gravely. "Your father and I are just of the same age. We were boys together. You know it, my dear."

She was a mere child, and he made her feel that she was. Her hands covered her face in an instant as she fled, and before the door had closed behind her, the colonel heard the first quick sob.

He had risen to his feet, and stood still, looking at the door. When he was alone, he might have smiled, as some men might have done, not at Sylvia, indeed, though at the absurdity of the situation. But his face was sad, and he quietly sat down again by the table, and began to think of what had happened.

Sylvia was very foolish, he said to himself, as he tried to impose upon his mind what he thought should have been his conviction. Yet he was deeply and truly touched by her half-childish love, and its innocence seemed pathetic to him, while he was hurt for her pain, and most of all for her overwhelming confusion.

At the same time came memories and visions, and his head sank forward a little as he sat in his chair by the table. The vision of hope was growing daily more dim, but the remembrance of the past was as undying as what has been is beyond recall.

Sylvia would wake from her girlish dream, and, in the fulness of young womanhood, would love a man of her own years. The colonel knew that. She would see that he was going in under the gateway of old age, while she was on the threshold of youth's morning. A few days, or a few months, or, at most, a few years more, and she must see that he was an old man. That was certain.

He sighed, not for Sylvia, but because age is that deadly sickness of which hope must perish at last. Time is a prince of narrow possessions, absolute where he reigns at all, cruel upon his people, and relentless; for, beyond his scanty principality, he is nothing, and his name is not known in the empire of eternity. Therefore while he rules he raises the dark standard of death, taking tribute of life, and giving back a slow poison in return.

Colonel Wimpole was growing old, and, though

the woman he still loved was not young, she was far younger than he, and he must soon seem an old man even in her eyes. And then there would not be much hope left. Sadly he wondered what Sylvia saw in him which that other woman, who had known him long, seemed to have never quite seen. But such questioning could find no satisfaction.

He might have remained absorbed in his reflexions for a long time had he been left alone, but the door opened behind him, and he knew by the steady and precise way in which it was opened and shut that his sister had entered the room.

"Richard," she said, "I am surprised." Then she stood still and waited.

Miss Wimpole was older than her brother, and was an exaggeration of him in petticoats. Her genuine admiration for him was curiously tempered by the fact that, when they had been children, she, as the elder, had kept him out of mischief, occasionally by force, often by authority, but never by persuasion. When in pinafores the colonel had been fond of sweets. Miss Wimpole considered that he owed his excellent health to her heroic determination to save him from destruction by jam. Since those days she had been obliged to yield to him on other points, but the memory of victory in the matter of preserves still made her manner authoritative.

c

She was very like him, being tall, thin, and not ungraceful, though as oddly precise in her movements and gestures as she was rigid in her beliefs, faithful in her affections, and just in her judgments. She had loved a man who had been killed in the civil war, and, being what she was, she had never so much as considered the possibility of marrying any one else. She was much occupied in good works and did much good, but she was so terribly accurate about it as to make Sylvia say that she was like a public charity that had been brought up in good society.

The colonel rose as she spoke.

"What is the matter?" he asked. "Why are you surprised?"

"What have you been saying to Sylvia, Richard?" enquired Miss Wimpole, not moving.

It would have been hard to hit upon a question more certain to embarrass the colonel. He felt the difficulty of his position so keenly that, old as he was, a faint colour rose in his cheeks. No answer occurred to him, and he hesitated.

"She has locked herself up in her room," continued Miss Wimpole, with searching severity, "and she is crying as though her heart would break. I heard her sobbing as I passed the door, and she would not let me in."

"I am very sorry," said the colonel, gravely.

"You do not seem much concerned," retorted

his sister. "I insist upon knowing what is the matter."

"Girls often cry," observed Colonel Wimpole, who felt obliged to say something, though he did not at all know what to say.

"Sylvia does not often cry, Richard, and you know it. You must have said something very unkind to her."

"I hope not," answered the colonel, evasively.

"Then why is she sobbing there, all by herself? I should like you to answer that question."

"I am very sorry that I cannot. When she is herself again you had better ask her."

Colonel Wimpole thought this good diplomacy. Since he meant not to tell his sister the truth, and was incapable of inventing a falsehood, he saw no means of escape except by referring Miss Wimpole directly to Sylvia.

"Richard," said the maiden lady, impressively, "I am surprised at you." And she turned away rather stiffly. "I thought you had more confidence in me," she added, as she reached the door.

But Colonel Wimpole made no further answer, for he saw that she had accepted his silence, which was all he wanted. When he was quite sure that she was in her own room, he went and got his hat and stick and slipped quietly out of the hotel.

CHAPTER II

COLONEL WIMPOLE did not like Lucerne, and as he strolled along the shady side of the street, he unconsciously looked up at the sky or down at the pavement rather than at the houses and the people. He disliked the tourists, the buildings, the distant scenery and the climate, and could give a reason for each separate aversion. Excepting the old tower, which was very much like a great many other old towers, he maintained that the buildings were either flat and dull, or most modernly pretentious. The tourists were tourists, and that alone condemned them beyond redemption. The climate was detestable, and he was sure that every one must think so. As for the scenery, with its prim lake, its tiresome snow mountains, and its toy trees, he said that it was little better than a perpetual chromolithograph, though at sunset it occasionally rose to the dignity of a transparent 'landscape' lamp-shade. The colonel's views of places were not wholly without prejudice. Being a very just man, where men and women were concerned, he allowed himself to be as unfair as he chose about inanimate things, from snow mountains to objects of art.

It was the pretension of Switzerland, he said, to please and to attract. Since it neither attracted him nor pleased him, he could not see what harm there could be in saying so. The Rigi's feelings could not be hurt by a sharp remark, nor could Mount Pilatus be supposed to be sensitive. He never abused Switzerland where any Swiss person could hear him. The same things, he said, were true of objects of art. If they failed to please, there could be no reason for their existence, or for not saying so, provided that the artist were not present. As for the latter, the charitable colonel was always willing to admit that he had done his best. It was gratuitous to suppose that any man should wilfully do badly what he could do well.

The colonel strolled slowly through the back streets, keeping in the shade. The day was hot, and he felt something like humiliation at having allowed himself to yield to circumstances and come out of the house earlier than usual. He would certainly not have acknowledged that he had been driven from the hotel by the fear of his sister's curiosity, but he would have faced a hotter sun rather than be obliged to meet her inquisitive questions again.

It was true that, being alone, he had to meet himself, and discuss with himself the painful little scene which had taken place that afternoon, for he was not one of those people who can get rid of unpleasant difficulties simply by refusing to think about them. And he examined the matter carefully as he went along, staring alternately at the sky and at the pavement, while his stick rang sharply in time with his light but still military step. He did not see the people who passed, but many of them looked at him, and noticed his face and figure, and set him down for a gentleman and an old soldier, as he was.

At first sight it seemed ridiculous that Sylvia should be in love with him; then it seemed sad, and then it seemed childish. He remembered the tragedy of Ninon de l'Enclos and her son, and it was horrible until he recalled an absurd story of a short-sighted young man who had fallen in love with his grandmother because his vanity would not allow him to wear spectacles. At this recollection, Colonel Wimpole smiled a little, though he was obliged to admit that Sylvia's eyes had always been very good. He wished, for a moment, that he were quite old already, instead of being only on the edge of old age. It would have been more easy to laugh at the matter. He was glad that he was not ten years younger, for in that case he might have been to blame. As he was turning into the main street, he caught sight of his own reflexion in the big plate glass window of a shop. He stopped short, with a painful sensation.

Had the image been that of a stranger, he should have judged the original to be a young man. The figure he saw was tall and straight and active, dressed in the perfection of neatness and good taste. The straw hat shaded the upper part of the face, but the sunlight caught the well-cut chin and gilded the small, closely trimmed moustache.

The colonel was extremely annoyed, just then, by his youthful appearance. He stopped and then went close to the plate glass window, till he could see his face distinctly in it, against the shadows of the darkened shop. He was positively relieved when he could clearly distinguish the fine lines and wrinkles and grey hairs, which he saw every morning in his mirror when he shaved. It was the sunshine playing with shadow that had called up the airy reflexion of his departed youth for a moment. Sylvia could never have seen him as he had appeared to himself in the window.

He looked a little longer. A lady in black was talking with the shopkeeper, and a short young man stood beside her. Colonel Wimpole's fingers tightened suddenly upon the familiar silver knob of his stick, his face grew a little pale, and he held his breath.

The lady turned quietly, walked to the window, followed by the shopkeeper and the young man, and pointed to a miniature which lay among a great number of more or less valuable antiquities and objects of art, all of them arranged so as to show them to an undue advantage. She stood quite still, looking down at the thing she wanted, and listening to what the shopkeeper said. The colonel, just on the other side of the thick plate glass, could hear nothing, though he could have counted the heavy lashes that darkly fringed the drooping lids as the lady kept her eyes upon the miniature. But his heart was standing still, for she was the woman he had loved so long and well, and he had not known that she was to pass through Lucerne. The short young man beside her was her son, and Colonel Wimpole knew him also, and had seen him from time to time during the nineteen years of his life. But he scarcely noticed him now, for his whole being was intent upon the face of the woman he loved.

She was dark, though her hair had never been jet black, and her complexion had always reminded the colonel of certain beautiful roses of which the smooth cream-coloured leaves are very faintly tinged with a warm blush that bears no relation to pink, but which is not red either, a tint without which the face was like marble, which could come in a moment but was long in fading as a northern sunset, and which gave wonderful life to the expression while it lasted. The lady's features were bold and well cut, but there were sad lines of lifelong weariness about the curved mouth and deep-set eyes; and there was a sort of patient but not weak sadness in all her bearing, the look of those who have tired but have not yielded, who have borne a calm face against a great trouble from without and a true heart against a strong temptation from within.

She was neither tall nor short, neither heavy nor light in figure, a woman of good and strong proportion, and she was dressed in black, though one small jewelled ornament and a coloured ribbon in her hat showed that she was not in mourning.

The elderly man at the window did not move as he watched her, for he felt sure that she must presently look up and meet his eyes. Then he would go in. But it did not happen just in that way, for her son recognized him first, a dark youth, very squarely built, with a heavy face and straight eyebrows that met over his nose. When he saw the colonel˙ he smiled, lifted his hat, and spoke to his mother. The lady started perceptibly and seemed to press the handle of her black parasol to her side. Several seconds passed after that, before the fringed lids were lifted, and the two looked at each other fixedly through the thick glass. A soft, slow smile smoothed and illuminated the lady's face, but Colonel Wimpole felt that he was paler than before, and his lips moved, unconsciously pronouncing a name which he had never spoken carelessly during two and twenty years. Nor, in that long time, had he ever met Helen Harmon suddenly, face to face, without feeling that his cheeks grew pale and that his heart stood still for a moment.

But his pulse beat quite regularly again when he had entered the shop and stood before her, extending his hand to meet hers, though he felt that he was holding out his heart to meet her heart, and he was full of unexpected happiness. So, in dim winter days, the sun shines out in a sudden glory, and spring is in the air before her time, for an hour; but afterwards it is cold again, and snow falls before night. Many a far glimpse of the flower-time had gladdened the colonel's heart before now, but the promised summer had never come.

The two stood still for a moment, hand in hand, and their eyes lingered in meeting, just a second or two longer than if they had been mere friends. That was all that a stranger could have seen to suggest that Richard Wimpole had loved Helen Harmon for twenty-two years, and the young man at her side did not even notice it. He shook hands with the colonel in his turn, and was the first to speak.

"One meets everybody in Lucerne," he observed, in a tactless generalization.

"I certainly did not hope to meet you," answered the colonel, smiling. "It is true that the cross-roads of Europe are at Lucerne if they are anywhere. My sister and I are taking Sylvia Strahan home from Japan. Of course we stopped here."

"Oh, of course!" laughed young Harmon. "Everybody stops here. We have been here ever so long, on our way to Carlsbad, I believe."

His mother glanced at him nervously before she spoke, as though she were not sure of what he might say next.

"I am thinking of buying a miniature," she said. "Will you look at it for me? You know all about these things. I should like your advice."

The dealer's face fell as he stood in the background, for he knew the colonel, and he understood English. But as she spoke, Mrs. Harmon was thinking more of Wimpole than of the miniature; and he, when he answered, was wondering how he could succeed in being alone with her for one half-hour — one of those little half-hours on which he lived for weeks and months after they were past.

Mrs. Harmon's manner was very quiet, and there was not often very much change in her expressions. Her laugh was low, regretful, and now and then a little bitter. Sometimes, when one might have expected a quick answer, she said nothing at all, and then her features had a calm immobility that was almost mysterious. Only now and then, when her son was speaking, she was evidently nervous, and at the sound of his voice her eyes turned quickly and nervously towards his face, while the shadows about the corners of her mouth deepened a little, and her lips set themselves. When he said anything more witless than usual, she was extraordinarily skilful and quick to turn his saying to sense by a clear explanation. At other times she generally spoke rather slowly and even indolently, as though nothing mattered very much. Yet she was a very sensible woman, and not by any means unpractical in daily life. Her tragedy, if it were one, had been slow and long drawn out.

First, a love which had been real, silent, and so altogether unsuspected, even by its object, that Richard Wimpole had never guessed it even to this day. Then a marriage thrust upon her by circumstances, and which she had accepted at last in the highest nobility of honest purpose. After that, much suffering, most scrupulously covered up from the world, and one moment of unforgotten horror. There was a crooked scar on her forehead, hidden by the thick hair which she drew down over it. When she was angry it turned red, though there was no other change in her face. Then a little while, and her husband's mind had gone. Even then she had tried to take care of him, until it had been hopeless, and he had become dangerous. The mercy of death seemed far from him, and he still lived, for he was very strong. And all along there had been the slowly increasing certainty of another misfortune. Her son, her only child, had been like other children at first, then dull and backward, and in the end, as compared with grown men, deficient. His mind had not developed much beyond a boy's; but he was unusually strong, he had learned to apply his strength, and had always excelled in athletic sports. One might have been deceived at first by the sharp glance of his eyes, but they were not bright with intelligence. The young man's perfect physical health alone made them clear and keen as a young animal's; but what they saw produced little reaction of understanding or thought.

Nor was that all that Helen Harmon had borne. There was one other thing, hardest of any to bear. By an accident she had learned at last that Richard Wimpole had loved her, and she had guessed that he loved her still. He had fancied her indifferent to him; and Harmon had been his friend in young days. Harmon had been called fast, even then, but not vicious, and he had been rich. Wimpole had stood aside and had let him win, being diffident, and really believing that it might be better for Helen in the end. He thought that she could make anything she chose of Harmon, who was furiously in love with her.

So the two had made the great mistake, each meaning to do the very best that could be done. But when Harmon had gone mad at last, and was in an asylum without prospect of recovery, and Helen found herself the administrator of his property for her son, it had been necessary to go through all his disordered papers, and she had found a letter of Wimpole's to her husband, written long ago. Had it been a woman's letter, she would have burned it unread. But it was a duty to read every paper which might bear upon business matters, from the beginning, and she naturally supposed that Harmon must have had some reason for keeping this one. So she read it.

It had been written in the early days of her husband's courtship. He, too, had been generous, then, with impulses of honour in which there had been, perhaps, something of vanity, though they had impelled him to do right. There had been some conversation between the friends, and Harmon had found out that Wimpole loved Helen. Not being yet so far in love as he was later, he had offered to go away and let the young colonel have a chance, since the latter had loved her first. Then Wimpole had written this letter which she found twenty years later.

It was simple, grateful, and honourably conceived. It said what he had believed to be the truth, that Helen did not care for him, that Harmon was quite as good as he in all ways, and much richer, and it finally and definitely refused the offer of 'a chance.' There was nothing tragic about it, nor any high-flown word in its short, clear phrases. But it had decided three lives, and the finding of it after such a long time hurt Helen more than anything had ever hurt her before.

In a flash she saw the meaning of Wimpole's life, and she knew that he loved her still, and had always loved her, though in all their many meetings, throughout those twenty years, he had never said one word of it to her. In one sudden comprehension, she saw all his magnificent generosity of silence. For he had partly known how Harmon had treated her. Every one knew something of it, and he must have known more than any one except the lawyer and the doctor whom she had been obliged to consult.

And yet, in that quick vision, she remembered, too, that she had never complained to him, nor ever said a word against Harmon. What Wimpole knew, beyond some matters of business in which he had helped her, he had learned from others or had guessed. But he had guessed much. Little actions of his, under this broad light of truth, showed her now that he had often understood what was happening when she had thought him wholly in ignorance.

But he, on his side, found no letter, nor any unexpected revelation of her secret; and still, to him, she seemed only to have changed indifference for friendship, deep, sincere, lasting and calm.

She kept the old letter two days, and then, when she was alone, she read it again, and her eyes filled, and she saw her hands bringing the discoloured page towards her lips. Then she started and looked at it, and she felt the scar on her forehead burning hot under her hair, and the temptation was great, though her anger at herself was greater. Harmon was alive, and she was a married woman, though he was a madman. She would not kiss the letter, but she laid it gently upon the smouldering embers, and then turned away, that she might not see it curling and glowing and blackening to ashes on the coals. That night a note from the director of the asylum told her that her husband was in excellent bodily health, without improvement in his mental condition. It was dated on the first of the month.

After that she avoided the colonel for some time, but when she met him her face was again like marble, and only the soft, slow smile and the steady, gentle voice showed that she was glad to see him. Two years had passed since then, and he had not even guessed that she knew.

He often sought her, when she was within reach of him, but their meeting to-day, in the fashionable antiquary's shop, at the cross-roads of Europe, was altogether accidental, unless it were brought about by the direct intervention of destiny. But who believes in destiny nowadays? Most people smile at the word 'fate,' as though it had no meaning at all. Yet call 'fate' the 'chemistry of the universe' and the sceptic's face assumes an expression of abject credulity, because the term has a modern ring and smacks of science. What is the difference between the two? We know a little chemistry: we can get something like the perfume of spring violets out of nauseous petroleum, and a flavour of strawberries out of stinking coal-tar; but we do not know much of the myriad natural laws by which our bodies are directed hither and thither, mere atoms in the everlasting whirlpool of all living beings. What can it matter whether we call those rules chemistry or fate? We shall submit to them in the end, with our bodies, though our souls rebel against them ever so eternally. The things that matter are quite different, and the less they have to do with our bodies, the better it is for ourselves.

Colonel Wimpole looked at the miniature and saw that it was a modern copy of a well-known French one, ingeniously set in an old case, to fit which it had perhaps been measured and painted. He looked at the dealer quickly, and the man expressed his despair by turning up his eyes a very little, while he bent his head forward and spread out his palms, abandoning the contest, for he recognized the colonel's right to advise a friend.

"What do you think of it?" asked Mrs. Harmon.

"That depends entirely on what you mean to do with it, and how much you would give for it," answered the colonel, who would not have let her buy an imitation under any circumstances, but was far too kind-hearted to ruin the shopkeeper in her estimation.

"I rather liked it," was the answer. "It was for myself. There is something about the expression that pleases me. The lady looks so blindly happy and delighted with herself. It is a cheerful little thing to look at."

The colonel smiled.

"Will you let me give it to you?" he asked, putting it into her hand. "In that way I shall have some pleasure out of it, too."

Mrs. Harmon held it for a moment, and looked at him thoughtfully, asking herself whether there was any reason why she should not accept the little present. He was not rich, but she had understood from his first answer that the thing was not worth much, after all, and she knew that he would not pay an absurd price for it. Her fingers closed quietly upon it.

"Thank you," she said. "I wanted it."

"I will come back this afternoon and pay for it," said the colonel to the dealer, as the three went out of the shop together a few moments later.

During the little scene, young Harmon had looked on sharply and curiously, but had not spoken.

"How are those things made, mother?" he asked, when they were in the street.

"What things?" asked Mrs. Harmon, gently.

"Those things — what do you call them? Like what Colonel Wimpole just gave you. How are they made?"

"Oh, miniatures? They are painted on ivory with very fine brushes."

"How funny! Why do they cost so much money, then?"

His questions were like those of a little child, but his mother's expression did not change as she answered him, always with the same unvarying gentleness.

"People have to be very clever to paint them," she said. "That is why the very good ones are worth so much. It is like a good tailor, my dear, who is paid well because he makes good coats, whereas the man who only knows how to make workmen's jackets earns very little."

"That's not fair," said young Harmon. "It isn't the man's fault if he is stupid, is it?"

"No, dear, it isn't his fault, it's his misfortune."

It took the young man so long to understand this that he said nothing more, trying to think over his mother's words, and getting them by heart, for they pleased him. They walked along in the hot sun and then crossed the street opposite the Schweizerhof to reach the shade of the foolish-looking trees that have been stuck about like Nuremberg toys, between the lake and the highway. The colonel had not spoken since they had left the shop.

"How well you are looking," he said suddenly, when young Harmon had relapsed into silence. "You are as fresh as a rose."

"A rose of yesterday," said Helen Harmon, a little sadly.

Quite naturally, Colonel Wimpole sighed as he walked along at her elbow; for though he did not know that she had ever loved him, he remembered the letter he had written to the man she had afterwards married, and he was too much a man himself not to believe that all might have been different if he had not written it.

"Where are you stopping?" he asked, when they had gone a few steps in silence.

Mrs. Harmon named a quiet hotel on the other side of the river.

"Close to us," observed the colonel, just as they reached the new bridge.

They were half-way across when an exclamation from young Harmon interrupted their conversation, which was, indeed, but a curiously stiff exchange of dry information about themselves and their movements, past, planned, and probable. For people who are fond of each other and meet rarely are first of all anxious to know when they may meet again. But the boy's cry of surprise made them look round.

"Jukes!" he exclaimed loudly. "Jukes!" he repeated, more softly but very emphatically, as though solely for his own benefit.

'Jukes' was his only expression when pleased and surprised. No one knew whether he had ever heard the word, or had invented it, and no one could ever discover what it meant nor from what it was derived. It seemed to be what Germans call a 'nature-sound,' by which he gave vent to his feelings. His mother hated it, but had never been able to induce him to substitute anything else in its place. She followed the direction of his eager glance, for she knew by his tone that he wanted what he saw.

She expected to see a pretty boat, or a big dog, or a gorgeous posted bill. Archie had a passion for the latter, and he often bought them and took them home with him to decorate his own particular room. He loved best the ones printed in violent and obtrusive colours. The gem of his collection was a purple woman on a red ground with a wreath of yellow flowers.

But Mrs. Harmon saw neither advertisement

nor dog, nor boat. She saw Sylvia Strahan. She knew the girl very well, and knew Miss Wimpole, of course. The two were walking along on the other side of the bridge, talking together. Against the blaze of the afternoon sun, reflected from the still lake, they could hardly have recognized the colonel and the Harmons, even if they had looked that way.

"It's Sylvia, mother," said Archie, glaring at the girl. "But isn't she grown! And isn't she lovely? Oh, Ju-u-ukes!"

His heavy lips thickened outwards as he repeated the mysterious ejaculation, and there was more colour than usual in his dark face. He was but little older than Sylvia, and the two had played together as small children, but he had never shown any special preference for her as a playmate. What struck him, now, was evidently her beauty. There was a look in his eyes, and a sort of bristling of the meeting eyebrows that reminded Helen of his father, and her white lids quivered for an instant at the recollection, while she felt a little chill run through her.

The colonel also saw.

"Shall we cross over and speak to them?" he asked in a low voice. "Or shall we just go on?"

"Let us go on," answered Helen. "I will

go and see them later. Besides, we have passed them now. Let us go on and get into the shade; it is dreadfully hot here."

"Won't you stop and speak to them, mother?" asked Archie Harmon, in a tone of deep disappointment. "Why, we have not seen them for ever so long!"

"We shall see them by and by," answered his mother. "It's too hot to go back now."

The young man turned his head and lagged a little, looking after the girl's graceful figure, till he stumbled awkwardly against a curbstone. But he did not protest any more. In his dull way, he worshipped his mother as a superior being, and hitherto he had always obeyed her with a half-childish confidence. His arrested intelligence still saw her as he had seen her ten years earlier, as a sort of high and protecting wisdom incarnate for his benefit, able to answer all questions and to provide him with unlimited pocket-money wherewith to buy bright-coloured posters and other gaudy things that attracted him. Up to a certain point, he could be trusted to himself, for he was almost as far from being an idiot as he was from being a normally thinking man. He was about as intelligent and about as well informed as a rather unusually dull schoolboy of twelve years or thereabouts. He did not lose his way in the streets, nor drop his money out of his pockets, and he could speak a little French and German which he had learned from a foreign nurse, enough to buy a ticket or order a meal. But he had scarcely outgrown toys, and his chief delight was to listen to the stories his mother told him. She was not very inventive, and she told the same old ones year after year. They always seemed to be new to him. He could remember faces and names fairly well, and had an average recollection of events in his own life; but it was impossible to teach him anything from books, his handwriting was the heavy, unformed scrawl of a child, and his spelling was one long disaster.

So far, at least, Helen had found only his intellectual deficiency to deal with, and it was at once a perpetual shame to her and a cause of perpetual sorrow and sympathy. But he was affectionate and docile enough, not cruel as some such beings are, and certainly not vicious, so far as she could see. Dull boys are rarely mischievous, though they are sometimes cruel, for mischief implies an imagination which dulness does not possess.

Archie Harmon had one instinct, or quality, which redeemed him from total insignificance and raised him above the level of an amiable and harmless animal. He had a natural horror of taking life, and felt the strongest possible impulse to save it at any risk to himself. His mother was never quite sure whether he made any distinction between the value of existence to a man, and its worth to an animal, or even to an insect. He seemed not to connect it with its possessor, but to look upon it as something to be preserved for its own sake, under all circumstances, wherever it manifested itself. At ordinary times he was sufficiently cautious for his own safety, and would hesitate to risk a fall or scratch in climbing, where most boys would have been quite unaware of such possibilities. But at the sight of any living thing in danger, a reckless instinct to save it took possession of him, and his sluggish nature was roused to sudden and direct activity, without any intermediate process of thought. He had again and again given proof of courage that might have shamed most men. He had saved a child from drowning in the North River, diving after it from a ferryboat running at full speed, and he had twice stopped bolting horses — once, a pair with a heavy brougham in the streets of New York, and once, in the park, a dog-cart driven by a lady. On the first of these two occasions he had been a good deal cut and bruised, and had narrowly escaped with his life. His mother was too brave not to be proud of his deeds, but with each one her fears for his own daily safety increased.

He was never violent, but he occasionally showed a strength that surprised her, though he never seemed to care about exhibiting it. Once, she had fallen and hurt her foot, and he had carried her up many stairs like a child. After that, she had felt now and then as men must feel who tame wild beasts and control them.

He worshipped her, and she saw that he looked with a sort of pity on other women, young or old, as not worthy to be compared with her in any way. She had begun to hope that she might be spared the humiliation of ever seeing him in love, despised or pitied, as the case might be, by some commonplace, pretty girl with white teeth and pink cheeks. She feared that, and she feared lest he should some day taste drink, and follow his father's ways to the same ruin. But as yet he had been like a child.

It was no wonder that she shuddered when, as he looked at Sylvia Strahan, she saw something in his face which had never been there before and heard that queer word of his uttered in such a tone. She wondered whether Colonel Wimpole had heard and seen, too, and for some time the three walked on in silence.

"Will you come in?" asked Mrs. Harmon, as they reached the door of her hotel.

The colonel followed her to her little sitting-room, and Archie disappeared; for the conversation of those whom he still, in his own thoughts, regarded as 'grown-up people' wearied him beyond bearing.

"My dear friend," said Colonel Wimpole, when they were alone, "I am so very glad to see you!"

He held one of her hands in his while he spoke the conventional words, his eyes were a little misty, and there was a certain tone in his voice which no one but Helen Harmon had ever heard.

"I am glad, too," she said simply, and she drew away her hand from his with a sort of deprecation which he only half understood, for he only knew that half of the truth which was in himself.

They sat down as they had sat many a time in their lives, at a little distance from each other, and just so that each had to turn the head a little to face the other. It was easier to talk in that position because there was a secret between them, besides many things which were not secrets, but of which they did not wish to speak.

"It is terribly long since we last met," said the colonel. "Do you remember? I went to see you in New York the day before we started for Japan. You had just come back from the country, and your house was in confusion."

"Oh yes, I remember," replied Mrs. Harmon. "Yes, it is terribly long; but nothing is changed."

"Nothing?" The colonel meant to ask her about Harmon, and she understood.

"Nothing," she answered gravely. "There was no improvement when the doctor wrote, on the first of last month. I shall have another report in a day or two. But they are all exactly alike. He will just live on, as he is now, to the end of his life."

"To the end of his life," repeated the colonel, in a low voice, and the two turned their heads and looked at each other.

"He is in perfect health," said Mrs. Harmon, looking away again.

She drew out a long hat-pin and lifted her hat from her head with both hands, for it was a hot afternoon, and she had come into the sitting-room as she was. The colonel noticed how neatly and carefully she did the thing. It seemed almost unnecessary to do it so slowly.

"It is so hot," she said, as she laid the hat on the table.

She was pale now, perhaps with the heat of which she complained, and he saw how tired her face was.

"Is this state of things really to go on?" he asked suddenly.

She moved a little, but did not look at him.

"I am not discontented," she said. "I am not — not altogether unhappy."

"Why should you not be released from it all?" asked the colonel.

It was the first time he had ever suggested such a possibility, and she looked away from him.

"It is not as if it had all been different before he lost his mind," he went on, seeing that she did not answer at once. "It is not as if you had not had fifty good reasons for a divorce before he finally went mad. What is the use of denying that?"

"Please do not talk about a divorce," said Mrs. Harmon, steadily.

"Please forgive me, if I do, my dear friend," returned the colonel, almost hotly; for he was suddenly convinced that he was right, and when he was right it was hard to stop him. "You have spent half your life in sacrificing all of yourself. Surely you have a right to the other half. There is not even the excuse that you might still do him some good by remaining his wife in name. His mind is gone, and he could not recognize you if he saw you."

"What should I gain by such a step, then?" asked Helen, turning upon him rather suddenly. "Do you think I would marry again?" There was an effort in her voice. "I hate to talk in this way, for I detest the idea of divorce, and the principle of it, and all its consequences. I believe it is going to be the ruin of half the world, in the end. It is a disgrace, in whatever way you look at it!"

"A large part of the world does not seem to think so," observed the colonel, rather surprised by her outbreak, though in any case excepting her own he might have agreed with her.

"It would be better if the whole world thought so," she observed with energy. "Do you know what divorce means in the end? It means the abolition of marriage laws altogether; it means reducing marriage to a mere experiment which may last a few days, a few weeks, or a few months, according to the people who try it. There are men and women, already, who have been divorced and married again half a dozen times. Before the next generation is old that will be the rule and not the exception."

"Dear me!" exclaimed Colonel Wimpole. "I hope not!"

"I know you agree with me," said Mrs. Harmon, with conviction. "You only argue on the other side because —" She stopped short.

"Why?" He did not look at her as he asked the question.

"Because you are my best friend," she answered, after a moment's hesitation, "and because you have got it into your head that I should be happier. I cannot imagine why. It would make no difference at all in my life — now."

The last word fell from her lips with a regretful tone and lingered a little on the air like the sad singing of a bell's last note, not broken by a following stroke. But the colonel was not satisfied.

"It may make all the difference, even now," he said. "Suppose that Harmon were to recover."

Helen did not start, for the thought had been long familiar to her, but she pressed her lips together a little and let her head rest against the back of her chair, half closing her eyes.

"It is possible," continued the colonel. "You know as well as I do that doctors are not always right, and there is nothing about which so little is really certain as insanity."

"I do not think it is possible."

"But it is, nevertheless. Imagine what it would be, if you began to hear that he was better and better, and finally well, and, at last, that there was no reason for keeping him in confinement."

Mrs. Harmon's eyes were quite closed now, as she leaned back. It was horrible to her to wish that her husband might remain mad till he died, yet she thought of what her own life must be if he should recover. She was silent, fighting it out in her heart. It was not easy. It was hard even to see what she should wish, for every human being has a prime right of self-preservation, against which no argument avails, save that of a divinely good and noble cause to be defended. Yet the moral wickedness of praying that Harmon might be a madman all the rest of his life frightened her. Throughout twenty years and more she had faced suffering and shame without flinching and without allowing herself one thought of retaliation or hatred. She had been hardened to the struggle and was not a woman to yield, if it should begin again, but she shrank from it, now, as the best and bravest may shrink at the thought of torture, though they would not groan in slow fire.

"Just think what it might be," resumed Colonel Wimpole. "Why not look the facts in the face while there is time? If he were let out, he would come back to you, and you would receive him, for I know what you are. You would think it right to take him back because you promised long ago to love, honour, and obey him. To love, to honour, and to obey — Henry Harmon!"

The colonel's steady grey eyes flashed for an instant, and his gentle voice was suddenly thick and harsh as he pronounced the last words. They meant terribly much to the woman who heard them, and in her distress she leaned forward in her seat and put up her hands to her temples, as though she had pain, gently pushing back the heavy hair she wore so low on her forehead. Wimpole had never seen her so much moved, and the gesture itself was unfamiliar to him. He did not remember to have ever seen her touch her hair with her hands, as some women do. He watched her now, as he continued to speak.

"You did all three," he said. "You honoured him, you loved him, and you obeyed him for a good many years. But he neither loved, nor honoured, nor cherished you. I believe that is the man's part of the contract, is it not? And marriage is always called a contract, is it not? Now, in any contract, both parties must do what they have promised, so that if one party fails, the other is not bound. Is not that true? And, Heaven knows, Harmon failed badly enough!"

"Don't! Please don't take it that way! No, no, no! Marriage is not a contract; it is a bond, a vow — something respected by man because it is sacred before God. If Henry failed a thousand times more, I should be just as much bound to keep my promise."

Her head sank still more forward, and her hands pushed her hair straight back from the temples.

"You will never persuade me of that," answered the colonel. "You will never make me believe—" He stopped short, for as he watched her, he saw what he had never seen before, a deep and crooked scar high on her forehead. "What is that?" he asked suddenly, leaning towards her, his eyes fixed on the ugly mark.

She started, stared at him, dropping her hands, realized what he had seen, and then instantly turned away. He could see that her fingers trembled as she tried to draw her hair down again. It was not like her to be vain, and he guessed at once that she had some reason other than vanity for hiding the old wound.

"What is that scar?" he asked again, determined to have an answer. "I never saw it before."

"It is a—I was hurt long ago—" She hesitated, for she did not know how to lie.

"Not so very long ago," said the colonel. "I know something about scars, and that one is not many years old. It does not look as though you had got it in a fall either. Besides, if you had, you would not mind telling me, would you?"

"Please don't ask me about it! I cannot tell you about it."

The colonel's face was hardening quickly. The lines came out in it stern and straight, as when, at evening, a sudden frost falls upon a still water, and the first ice-needles shoot out, clear and stiff. Then came the certainty, and Wimpole looked as he had looked long ago in battle.

"Harmon did that," he said at last, and the wrathful thought that followed was not the less fierce because it was unspoken.

Helen's hands shook now, for no one had ever known how she had been wounded. But she said nothing, though she knew that her silence meant her assent. Wimpole rose suddenly, straight as a rifle, and walked to the window, turning his back upon her. He could say things there, under his breath, which she could not understand, and he said them, earnestly.

"He did not know what he was doing," Helen said, rather unsteadily.

The colonel turned on his heels at the window, facing her, and his lips still moved slowly, though no words came. Helen looked at him and knew that she was glad of his silent anger. Not realizing what she was thinking of, she wondered what sort of death Harmon might have died if Richard Wimpole had seen him strike her to the ground with a cut-glass decanter. For a moment the cloak of mercy and forgiveness was rent from head to heel. The colonel would have killed the man with those rather delicate looking hands of his, talking to him all the time in a low voice. That was what she thought, and perhaps she was not very far wrong. Even now, it was well for Harmon that he was safe in his asylum on the other side of an ocean.

It was some time before Wimpole could speak. Then he came and stood before Helen.

"You will stay a few days? You do not mean to go away at once?" he said, with a question.

"Yes."

"Then I think I shall go away now, and come and see you again later."

He took her hand rather mechanically and left the room. But she understood and was grateful.

CHAPTER III

WHEN Archie Harmon disappeared and left the colonel and his mother together, she supposed that he had gone to his room to sleep, for he slept a great deal, or to amuse himself after his fashion, and she did not ask him where he was going. She knew what his favourite amusement was, though he did his best to keep it a secret from her.

There was a certain mysterious box, which he had always owned, and took everywhere with him, and of which he always had the key in his pocket. It took up a good deal of space, but he could never be persuaded to leave it behind when they went abroad.

To-day he went to his room, as usual, locked the door, took off his coat, and got the box out of a corner. Then he sat down on the floor and opened it. He took out some child's building-blocks, some tin soldiers, much the worse for wear, for he was ashamed to buy new ones, and a small and gaudily painted tin cart, in which an impossible lady and gentleman of papier-mâché, dressed in blue, grey, and yellow, sat leaning back with folded arms and staring, painted eyes. There were a few other toys besides, all packed away with considerable neatness, for Archie was not slovenly.

He sat cross-legged on the floor, a strong grown man of nearly twenty years, and began to play with his blocks. His eyes fixed themselves on his occupation, as he built up a little gateway with an arch and set red-legged French soldiers on each side of it for sentinels. He had played the same game a thousand times already, but the satisfaction had not diminished. One day in a hotel he had forgotten to lock the door, and his mother had opened it by mistake, thinking it was that of her own room. Before he could look round she had shut it again, but she had seen, and it had been like a knife-thrust. She kept his secret, but she lost heart from that day. He was still a child, and was always to be one.

Yet there was perhaps something more of intelligence in the childish play than she had guessed. He was lacking in mind, but not an idiot; he sometimes said and did things which were certainly far beyond the age of toys. Possibly the attraction lay in a sort of companionship which he felt in the society of the blocks, and the tin soldiers, and the little papier-mâché lady and gentleman. He felt that they understood what he meant and would answer him if they could speak, and would expect no more of him than he could give. Grown people always seemed to expect a great deal more, and looked at him strangely when he called Berlin the capital of Austria and asked why Brutus and Cassius murdered Alexander the Great. The toy lady and gentleman were quite satisfied if their necks were not broken in the cunningly devised earthquake which always brought the block house down into a heap when he had looked at it long enough and was already planning another.

Besides, he did all his best thinking among his toys, and had invented ways of working out results at which he could not possibly have arrived by a purely mental process. He could add and subtract, for instance, with the bits of wood, and, by a laborious method, he could even do simple multiplication, quite beyond him with paper and pencil. Above all, he could name the tin soldiers after people he had met, and make them do anything he pleased, by a sort of rudimentary theatrical instinct that was not altogether childish.

To-day he built a house as usual, and, as usual, after some reflexion as to the best means of ruining it by taking out a single block, he pulled it down with a crash. But he did not at once begin another. On the contrary, he sat looking at the ruins for a long time in a rather disconsolate way, and then all at once began to pack all the toys into the box again.

"I don't suppose it matters," he said aloud. "But of course Sylvia would think me a baby if she saw me playing with blocks."

And he made haste to pack them all away, locking the box and putting the key into his pocket. Then he went and looked through the half-closed blinds into the sunny street, and he could see the new bridge not far away.

"I don't care what mother thinks!" he exclaimed. "I'm going to find her again."

He opened his door softly, and a moment later he was in the street, walking rapidly towards the bridge. At a distance he looked well. It was only when quite near to him that one was aware of an undefinable ungainliness in his face and figure — something blank and meaningless about him, that suggested a heavy wooden doll dressed in good clothes. In military countries one often receives that impression. A fine-looking infantry soldier, erect, broad shouldered, bright eyed, spotless, and scrupulously neat, comes marching along and excites one's admiration for a moment. Then, when close to him, one misses something which ought to go with such manly bearing. The fellow is only a country lout, perhaps, hardly able to read or write, and possessed of an intelligence not much beyond the highest development of instinct. Drill, exercise, and the fear of black bread and water under arrest, have produced a fine piece of military machinery, but they could not create a mind, nor even the appearance of intelligence, in the wooden face. In a year or two the man will lay aside his smart uniform and go back to the class whence he came. One may give iron the shape and general look of steel, but not the temper and the springing quality.

Archie Harmon looked straight ahead of him as he crossed the bridge and followed the long street that runs beside the water, past the big hotels and the gaudy awnings of the provincially smart shops. At first he only looked along the pavement, searching among the many people who passed. Then as he remembered how Colonel Wimpole had seen him through a shop window, he stopped before each of the big plate glass ones and peered curiously into the shadows within.

At last, in a milliner's, he saw Sylvia and Miss Wimpole, and his heavy face grew red, and his eyes glared oddly as he stood motionless outside, under the awning, looking in. His

lips went out a little, as he pronounced his own
especial word very softly.

"Jukes!"

He stood first on one foot and then on the
other, like a boy at a pastry cook's, hesitating,
while devouring with his eyes. He could see
that Sylvia was buying a hat. She turned a
little each way as she tried it on before a big
mirror, putting up her hands and moving her
arms in a way that showed all the lines of her
perfect figure.

Archie went in. He had been brought up by
his mother, and chiefly by women, and he had
none of that shyness about entering a women's
establishment, like a milliner's, which most boys
and many men feel so strongly. He walked in
boldly and spoke as soon as he was within
hearing.

"Miss Sylvia! I say! Miss Sylvia — don't
you know me?"

The question was a little premature, for Sylvia had barely caught sight of him when he
asked it. When she had recognized him, she
did not look particularly pleased.

"It's poor Archie Harmon, my dear," said
Miss Wimpole, in a low voice, but quite audibly.

"Oh, I have not forgotten you!" said Sylvia,
trying to speak pleasantly as she gave her
hand. "But where in the world did you come

from? And what are you doing in a milliner's shop?"

"I happened to see you through the window, so I just came in to say how do you do. There's no harm in my coming in, is there? You look all right. You're perfectly lovely."

His eyes were so bright that Sylvia felt oddly uncomfortable.

"Oh no," she answered, with an indifference she did not feel. "It's all right — I mean — I wish you would go away now, and come and see us at the hotel, if you like, by and by."

"Can't I stay and talk to you? Why can't I stay and talk to her, Miss Wimpole?" he asked, appealing to the latter. "I want to stay and talk to her. We are awfully old friends, you know; aren't we, Sylvia? You don't mind my calling you Sylvia, instead of Miss Sylvia, do you?"

"Oh no! I don't mind that!" Sylvia laughed a little. "But do please go away now!"

"Well — if I must — " he broke off, evidently reluctant to do as she wished. "I say," he began again with a sudden thought, "you like that hat you're trying on, don't you?"

Instantly Sylvia, who was a woman, though a very young one, turned to the glass again, settled the hat on her head and looked at herself critically.

"The ribbons stick up too much, don't they?" she asked, speaking to Miss Wimpole, and quite forgetting Archie Harmon's presence. "Yes, of course they do! The ribbons stick up too much," she repeated to the milliner in French.

A brilliant idea had struck Archie Harmon. He was already at the desk, where a young woman in black received the payments of passing customers with a grieved manner.

"She says the ribbons stick up too much," he said to the person at the desk. "You get them to stick up just right, will you? The way she wants them. How much did you say the hat was? Eighty francs? There it is. Just say that it's paid for, when she asks for the bill."

The young woman in black raked in the note and the bits of gold he gave her, catching them under her hard, thin thumb on the edge of the desk, and counting them as she slipped them into her little drawer. She looked rather curiously at Archie, and there was still some surprise in her sour face when he was already on the pavement outside. He stopped under the awning again, and peered through the window for a last look at the grey figure before the mirror, but he fled precipitately when Sylvia turned as though she were going to look at him. He was thoroughly delighted with himself. It was just what Colonel Wimpole had done about the miniature, he thought; and then, a hat was so much more useful than a piece of painted ivory.

In a quarter of an hour he was in his own room again, sitting quite quietly on a chair by the window, and thinking how happy he was, and how pleased Sylvia must be by that time.

But Sylvia's behaviour when she found out what he had done would have damped his innocent joy, if he had been looking through the windows of the shop, instead of sitting in his own room. Her father, the admiral, had a hot temper, and she had inherited some of it.

"Impertinent young idiot!" she exclaimed, when she realized that he had actually paid for the hat, and the angry blood rushed to her face. "What in the world—" She could not find words.

"He is half-witted, poor boy," interrupted Miss Wimpole. "Take the hat, and I will manage to give his mother the money."

"Betty Foy and her idiot boy over again!" said Sylvia, with all the brutal cruelty of extreme youth. "'That all who view the idiot in his glory'—" As the rest of the quotation was not applicable, she stopped and stamped her little foot in speechless indignation.

"The young gentleman doubtless thought to give Mademoiselle pleasure," suggested the milliner, suavely. "He is doubtless a relation—"

"He is not a relation at all!" exclaimed Sylvia in English, to Miss Wimpole. "My relations are not idiots, thank Heaven! And it's the only one of all those hats that I could wear! Oh, Aunt Rachel, what shall I do? I can't possibly take the thing, you know! And I must have a hat. I've come all the way from Japan with this old one, and it isn't fit to be seen."

"There is no reason why you should not take this one," said Miss Wimpole, philosophically. "I promise you that Mrs. Harmon shall have the money by to-night, since she is here. Your Uncle Richard will go and see her at once, of course, and he can manage it. They are on terms of intimacy," she added rather primly, for Helen Harmon was the only person in the world of whom she had ever been jealous.

"You always use such dreadfully correct language, Aunt Rachel," answered the young girl. "Why don't you say that they are old friends? 'Terms of intimacy' sounds so severe, somehow."

"You seem impatient, my dear," observed Miss Wimpole, as though stating a fact about nature.

"I am," answered Sylvia. "I know I am.

You would be impatient if an escaped lunatic rushed into a shop and paid for your gloves, or your shoes, or your hat, and then rushed off again, goodness knows where. Wouldn't you? Don't you think I am right?"

"You had better tell them to send the hat to the hotel," suggested Aunt Rachel, not paying the least attention to Sylvia's appeal for justification.

"If I must take it, I may as well wear it at once, and look like a human being," said Sylvia. "That is, if you will really promise to send Mrs. Harmon the eighty francs at once."

"I promise," answered Miss Wimpole, solemnly, and as she had never broken her word in her life, Sylvia felt that the difficulty was at an end.

The milliner smiled sweetly, and bowed them out.

"All the same," said Sylvia, as she walked up the street with the pretty hat on her head, "it is an outrageous piece of impertinence. Idiots ought not to be allowed to go about alone."

"I should think you would pity the poor fellow," said Miss Wimpole, with a sort of severe kindliness, that was genuine but irritating.

"Oh yes! I will pity him by and by, when I'm not angry," answered the young girl. "Of course — it's all right, Aunt Rachel, and I'm not depraved nor heartless, really. Only, it was very irritating."

"You had better not say anything about it to your Uncle Richard, my dear. He is so fond of Archie's mother that he will feel very badly about it. I will break it to him gently."

"Would he?" asked Sylvia, in surprise. "About herself, I should understand — but about that boy! I can't see why he should mind."

"He 'minds,' as you call it, everything that has to do with Mrs. Harmon."

Sylvia glanced at her companion, but said nothing, and they walked on in silence for some time. It was still hot, for the sun had not sunk behind the mountains; but the street was full of people, who walked about indifferent to the temperature, because Switzerland is supposed to be a cold country, and they therefore thought that it was their own fault if they felt warm. This is the principle upon which nine people out of ten see the world when they go abroad. And there was a fine crop of European and American varieties of the tourist taking the air on that afternoon, men, women, and children. The men who had huge field-glasses slung over their shoulders by straps predominated, and one, by whom Sylvia was particularly struck, was arrayed in

F

blue serge knickerbockers, patent-leather walking-boots, and a very shiny high hat. But there were also occasional specimens of what she called the human being — men in the ordinary garments of civilization, and not provided with opera-glasses. There were, moreover, young and middle-aged women in short skirts, boots with soles half an inch thick, complexions in which the hue of the boiled lobster vied with the deeper tone of the stewed cherry, bearing alpenstocks that rang and clattered on the pavement; women who, in the state of life to which Heaven had called them, would have gone to Margate or Staten Island for a Sunday outing, but who had rebelled against providence, and forced the men of their families to bring them abroad. And the men generally walked a little behind them and had no alpenstocks, but carried shawls and paper bundles, badges of servitude, and hoped that they might not meet acquaintances in Lucerne, because their women looked like angry cooks and had no particular luggage. Now and then a smart old gentleman with an eyeglass, in immaculate grey or white, threaded his way along the pavement, with an air of excessive boredom; or a young couple passed by, in the recognizable newness of honeymoon clothes, the young wife talking perpetually, and evidently laughing at the ill-dressed women, while the equally young husband answered in monosyllables, and was visibly nervous lest his bride's remarks should be overheard and give offence.

Then there were children, obtrusively English children, taken abroad to be shown the miserable inferiority of the non-British world, and to learn that every one who had not yellow hair and blue eyes was a 'nasty foreigner,'—unless, of course, the individual happened to be English, in which case nothing was said about hair and complexion. And also there were the vulgar little children of the not long rich, repulsively disagreeable to the world in general, but pathetic in the eyes of thinking men and women. They are the sprouting shoots of the gold-tree, beings predestined never to enjoy, because they will be always able to buy what strong men fight for, and will never learn to enjoy what is really to be had only for money; and the measure of value will not be in their hands and heads, but in bank-books, out of which their manners have been bought with mingled affection and vanity. Surely, if anything is more intolerable than a vulgar woman, it is a vulgar child. The poor little thing is produced by all nations and races, from the Anglo-Saxon to the Slav. Its father was happy in the struggle that ended in success. When it grows old, its own children will perhaps be happy in the sort of refined existence which wealth can bring in the third generation. But the child of the man grown suddenly rich is a living misfortune between two happinesses: neither a worker nor an enjoyer; having neither the satisfaction of the one, nor the pleasures of the other; hated by its inferiors in fortune, and a source of amusement to its ethic and æsthetic betters.

Sylvia had never thought much about the people she passed in a crowd. Thought is generally the result of suffering of some kind, bodily or intellectual, and she had but little acquaintance with either. She had travelled much, and had been very happy until the present time, having been shown the world on bright days and by pleasant paths. But to-day she was not happy, and she began to wonder how many of the men and women in the street had what she had heard called a 'secret care.' Her eyes had been red when she had at last yielded to Miss Wimpole's entreaties to open the door, but the redness was gone already, and when she had tried on the hat before the glass she had seen with a little vanity, mingled with a little disappointment, that she looked very much as usual, after all. Indeed, there had been more than one moment when she had forgotten her troubles because the ribbons on the new hat stuck up too much. Yet she was really unhappy, and sad at heart. Perhaps some of the people she passed, even the women with red faces, dusty skirts, and clattering alpenstocks, were unhappy too.

She was not a foolish girl, nor absurdly romantic, nor full of silly sentimentalities, any more than she was in love with Colonel Wimpole in the true sense of the word. For she knew nothing of its real meaning, and, apart from that meaning, what she felt for him filled all the conditions proposed by her imagination. If one could classify the ways by which young people pass from childhood to young maturity, one might say that they are brought up by the head, by the imagination, or by the heart, and one might infer that their subsequent lives are chiefly determined by that one of the three which has been the leading-string. Sylvia's imagination had generally had the upper hand, and it had been largely fed and cultivated by her guardian, though quite unintentionally on his part. His love of artistic things led him to talk of them, and his chivalric nature found sources of enthusiasm in lofty ideals, while his own life, directed and moved as it was by a secret, unchanging and self-sacrificing devotion to one good woman, might have served as a model for any man. Modest, and not much inclined to think of himself, he did not realize that although the highest is quite beyond any one's reach, the search after it is always upward, and may lead a good man very far.

Sylvia saw the result, and loved it for its own sake with an attachment so strong that it made her blind to the more natural sort of humanity which the colonel seemed to have outgrown, and which, after all, is the world as we inherit it, to love it, or hate it, or be indifferent to it, but to live with it, whether we will or not. He fulfilled her ideal, because it was an ideal which he himself had created in her mind, and to which he himself nearly approached. Logically speaking, she was in a vicious circle, and she liked what he had taught her to like, but liked it more than he knew she did.

Sylvia glanced at Miss Wimpole sideways. She knew her simple story, and wondered whether she herself was to live the same sort of life. The idea rather frightened her, to tell the truth, for she knew the aridity of the elderly maiden lady's existence, and dreaded anything like it. But it was very simple and logical and actual. Miss Wimpole had loved a man who had been killed. Of course she had never married, nor ever thought of loving any one else. It was perfectly simple. And Sylvia loved, and was not loved, as she told herself, and she also must look forward to a perpetually grey life.

Then, suddenly, she felt how young she was, and she knew that the colonel was almost an old man, and her heart rebelled. But this seemed disloyal, and she blushed at the word 'unfaithful,' which spoke itself in her sensitive conscience with the cruel power to hurt which such words have against perfect innocence. Besides, it was as if she were quarrelling with what she liked, because she could not have it, and she felt as though she were thinking childishly, which is a shame in youth's eyes.

Also, she was nervous about meeting him again, for she had not seen him since she had fled from the room in tears, though he had seen her on the bridge. She wished that she might not see him at all for a whole day, at least, and that seemed a very long time.

Altogether, when she went into the hotel again, she was in a very confused state of mind and heart, and was beginning to wish that she had never been born. But that was childish, too.

CHAPTER IV

HELEN HARMON was glad when the colonel was gone. She went to a mirror, fixed to the wall between the two windows of the room, and she carefully rearranged her hair. She could not feel quite herself until she knew that the scar was covered again and hidden from curious eyes. Then she sat down, glad to be alone. It had been a great and unexpected pleasure to see Wimpole, but the discovery he had made, and the things he had said, had disturbed and unnerved her.

There had been conviction in his voice when he had said that Harmon might recover, and the possibility of a change in her husband's condition had crossed her mind more than once. She felt that a return to such a state of things as had made up her life before he had become insane, would kill her by slow torture. It was of no use any longer to tell herself that recovery was impossible, and to persuade herself that it was so by the mere repetition of the words. Words had no more weight, now.

She thought of her freedom since that merciful deliverance. It was not happiness, for there were other things yet to be suffered, but it was real freedom. She had her son's affliction to bear, but she could bear it alone and go and come with him as she pleased. She contrasted this liberty with what she had borne for years.

The whole history of their married life came back to her, the gradual progress of it from first to last, if indeed it had yet reached the end and was not to go back to the beginning again.

First there had been the sort of half-contented resignation which many young women feel during the early months of married life, when they have made what is called by the world a good match, simply because they saw no reason for not marrying and because they were ashamed to own that they cared for a man who did not seem to be attached to them. Sometimes the state lasts throughout life, a neutral, passionless, negative state, in which the heart turns flat and life is soon stale, a condition in which many women, not knowing what pain is, grow restless and believe that it must be pleasanter to be hurt than to feel nothing.

Henry Harmon had been handsome, full of life and nerve and enthusiasm for living, a rider, a sportsman, more reckless than brave and more brave than strong-minded, with a gift for being, or seeming to be, desperately in love, which had ultimately persuaded Helen to marry him in spite of her judgment. He turned pale when he was long near her, his eyes flashed darkly, his hands shook a little, and his voice trembled. An older woman might have thought it all rather theatrical, but he seemed to suffer, and that moved Helen, though it did not make her really love him. Women know that weakness of theirs and are more afraid of pitying an importunate suitor than of admiring him. So Helen married Harmon.

Disillusionment came as daylight steals upon dancers in a ballroom. At first it was not so painful as might have been imagined, for Helen was not excessively sensitive, and she had never really loved the man in the least. He grew tired of her and left her to herself a good deal. That was a relief, at first, for after she had realized that she did not love him, she shrank from him instinctively, with something very like real shame, and to be left alone was like being respected.

"Mrs. Blank's husband is neglecting her," says one.

"She does not seem to care; she looks very happy," answers another.

And she is temporarily happy, because Mr. Blank's neglect gives her a sense of bodily relief, for she knows that she has made a mistake in marrying him. It was so with Helen, and as she was not a changeable nor at all a capricious person, it might have continued to be so. But Harmon changed rapidly in the years that followed. From having been what people called fast, he became dissipated. He had always loved the excitement of wine. When it failed him, he took to stronger stuff, which presently became the essential requisite of his being. He had been said to be gay, then he was spoken of as wild, then as dissipated. Some people avoided him, and every one pitied Helen. Yet although he ruined his constitution, he did not wreck his fortunes, for he was lucky in all affairs connected with money. There remained many among his acquaintances who could not afford to disapprove of him, because he had power.

He drank systematically, as some men do, for the sake of daily excitement, and Helen learned to know tolerably well when he was dangerous and when he might be approached with safety. But more than once she had made horrible mistakes, and the memories of them were like dreams out of hell. In his drunkenness her face recalled other days to him, and forgotten words of passion found thick and indistinct utterance. Once she had turned on him, white and desperate in her self-defence. He struck her on the forehead with a cut-glass decanter, snatched from her toilet table. When she came to herself hours afterwards, it was daylight. Harmon was in a drunken sleep, and the blood on his face was hers.

She shuddered with pain from head to foot when she thought of it. Then had come strange lapses of his memory, disconnected speech, even hysterical tears, following senseless anger, and then he had ceased to recognize any one, and had almost killed one of the men who took care of him, so that it was necessary to take him to an asylum, struggling like a wild beast. Twice, out of a sense of duty, she had been to see whether he knew her, but he knew no one, and the doctors said it was a hopeless case. Since then she had received a simple confirmation of the statement every month, and there seemed to be no reason for expecting any change, and she felt free.

Free was the only word she could find, and she applied it to herself in a sense of her own, meaning that she had been liberated from the thraldom in which she had lived so many years face to face with his brutality, and hiding it from the world as best she could, protecting and defending his name, and refusing pity as she would have refused money had she been poor.

People might guess what she suffered, but no one should know it from her, and no one but herself could tell the half of what she underwent.

Yet, now that it was all over, Wimpole suggested that it might begin again, unless she took measures to defend herself. But her heart revolted at the idea of a divorce. She wondered, as she tried to test herself, whether she could be as strong if the case really arose. It never occurred to her to ask whether her strength might not be folly, for it lay in one of those convictions by which unusual characters are generally moved, and conviction never questions itself.

It was not that in order to be divorced she must almost necessarily bring up in public and prove by evidence a certain number of her many wrongs. The publicity would be horrible. Every newspaper in the country would print the details, with hideous head-lines. Even her son's deficiency would be dragged into the light. She should have to explain how she had come by the scar on her forehead, and much more that would be harder to tell, if she could bring her lips to speak the words.

Nevertheless, she could do that, and bear everything, for a good cause. If, for instance, Archie's future depended upon it, or even if it could do him some good, she could do all that for his sake. But even for his sake, she would not be divorced, not even if Harmon were let out of the asylum and came back to her.

Some people, perhaps many, could not understand such a prejudice, or conviction, now that all convictions are commonly spoken of as relative. But will those who do not understand Helen Harmon consider how the world looked upon divorce as recently as five and twenty years ago? Nothing can give a clearer idea of the direction taken by social morality than the way in which half the world has become accustomed to regard marriage as a contract, and not as a bond, during the lifetime of people now barely in middle age.

Twenty-five or thirty years ago divorces were so rare as to be regarded in the light of very uncommon exceptions to the general rule. The divorce law itself is not yet forty years old in England, nor twenty years old in France. In Italy there is no civil divorce whatever at the present day, and the Catholic Church only grants what are not properly divorces, but annullations of marriage, in very rare cases, and with the greatest reluctance.

Even in America, every one can remember how divorce was spoken of and thought of until very recently. Within a few years it was deemed to be something very like a disgrace, and certainly a profoundly cynical and immoral proceeding. To-day we can most of us count in our own acquaintance half a dozen persons who have been divorced and have married again. Whatever we may think of it in our hearts, or whatever our religious convictions may be on the subject, it has become so common that when we hear of a flagrant case of cruelty or unfaithfulness, by which a man or woman suffers, the question at once rises to our lips, 'Why does he not divorce his wife?' or 'Why does she not divorce her husband?' We have grown used to the idea, and, if it does not please us, it certainly does not shock us. It shocked our fathers, but we are perfectly indifferent.

Of course there are many, perhaps a majority, who, though not Roman Catholics, would in their own lives put up with almost anything rather than go to the divorce court for peace. Some actually suffer much and ask for no redress. But there are very many who have not suffered anything at all, excepting the favourite 'incompatibility of temper,' and who have taken advantage of the loose laws in certain states to try a second matrimonial experiment. In what calls itself society, there seems still to be a prejudice against a third marriage for divorced persons, but at the present rate of so-called progress this cannot last long, and the old significance of the word marriage will be quite lost before our great grandchildren are dead; in other words, by the end of the next century, at the furthest.

There are various forms of honourable political dreaming and of dishonourable political mischief-making nowadays, which we are accustomed to call collectively 'socialism.' Most of these rely for their hope of popular success upon their avowed intention of dividing property and preventing its subsequent accumulation. Marriage is an incentive of such accumulation, because it perpetuates families and therefore keeps property together by inheritance. Therefore most forms of socialism are at present in favour of divorce, as a means of ultimately destroying marriage altogether. A proverb says that whosoever desires the end, desires also the means. There is more truth in the saying than morality in the point of view it expresses. But there are those who desire neither the means nor the end to which they lead, and a struggle is coming, the like of which has not been seen since the beginning of the world, and of which we who are now alive shall not see the termination.

The Civil War in the United States turned upon slavery incidentally, not vitally. The cause of that great fight lay much deeper. In the same way the Social War, which is coming, will turn incidentally upon religion, and be perhaps called a religious war hereafter, but it will not be declared for the sake of faith against unbelief, nor be fought at first by any church, or alliance of churches, against atheism. It will simply turn out that the men who fight on the one side will have either the convictions or the prejudices of Christianity, or both, and that their adversaries will have neither. But the struggle will be at its height when the original steady current of facts which led to inevitable strife has sunk into apparent insignificance under the raging storm of conflicting belief and unbelief. The disadvantage of the unbelievers will lie in the fact that belief is positive and assertive, whereas unbelief is negative and argumentative. It is indeed easier to deny than to prove almost anything. But that is not the question. In life and war it is generally easier to keep than to take, and besides, those who believe 'care,' as we say, whereas those who deny generally 'care' very little. It is probable, to say the least of it, that so long as the socialists of the near future believe assertively that they have discovered the means of saving humanity from misery and poverty, and fight for a pure conviction, they will have the better of it, but that when they find themselves in the position of attacking half of mankind's religious faith, having no idea, but only a proposition, to offer in its place, they will be beaten.

That seems far from the question of divorce, but it is not. Before the battle, the opposing forces are encamped and intrenched at a little distance from each other, and each tries to undermine the other's outworks. Socialism, collectively, has dug a mine under Social Order's strongest tower, which is called marriage, and the edifice is beginning to shake from its foundations, even before the slow-match is lighted.

To one who has known the world well for a quarter of a century, it seems as though the would-be destroyers of the existing order had forgotten, among several other things, the existence of woman, remembering only that of the female. They practically propose to take away woman's privileges in exchange for certain more or less imaginary 'rights.' There is an apparent justice in the 'conversion,' as it would be called in business. If woman is to have all the rights of man, which, indeed, seem reducible to a political vote now and then, why should she keep all the privileges which man is not allowed? But tell her that when she is allowed to vote for the president of the United States once in four years, no man shall be expected to stand up in a public conveyance to give her a seat, nor to fetch and carry for her, nor to support her instead of being supported by her, nor to keep her for his wife any longer than he chooses, and the 'conversion' looks less attractive.

The reason why woman has privileges instead of rights is that all men tacitly acknowledge the future of humanity to be dependent on her from generation to generation. Man works or fights, and takes his rights in payment therefor, as well as for a means of working and fighting to greater advantage. And while he is fighting or working, his wife takes care of his children almost entirely. There is not one household in a hundred thousand, rich or poor, where there is really any question about that. It sounds insignificant, perhaps, and it looks as though anybody could take care of two or three small children. Those who have tried it know better, and they are women. Now and then rich mothers are too lazy to look after their children themselves. To do them such justice as one may, they are willing to spend any amount of money in order to get it well done for them, but the result is not encouraging to those who would have all children brought up 'by the state.' Even if it were so, who would bring them up? Women, of course. Then why not their own mothers? Because mothers sometimes—or often, for the sake of argument—do not exactly know how. Then educate the mothers, give them chances of knowing how, let them learn, if you know any better than they, which is doubtful, to say the least of it.

Moreover, does any man in his senses really believe that mothers, as a whole, would submit and let their children be taken from them to a state rearing-house, to be brought up under a number on a ticket by professional baby-farmers, in exchange for the 'right' to vote at a presidential election, and the 'right' to put away their husbands and take others as often as they please, and the 'right' to run for Congress? Yet the plan has been proposed gravely.

There seems to be a good deal to be said in favour of the existing state of things, after all, and particularly in favour of marriage, and therefore against divorce; and it is not surprising that woman, whose life is in reality far more deeply affected by both questions than man's life is, should have also the more profound convictions about them.

Woman brings us into the world, woman is our first teacher, woman makes the world what it is, from century to century. We can no more escape from woman, and yet continue to live our lives as they should be lived, than we can hide ourselves from nature. We are in her care or in her power during more than half our years, and often during all, from first to last. We are born of her, we grow of her, as truly as trees and flowers come of the mother earth and draw their life from the soil in which they are planted. The man who denies his mother is a bad man, and the man who has not loved woman is a man in darkness.

Man is not really unjust to woman in his thoughts of her either, unless he be a lost soul, but he has not much reason in respect of her nor any justice in his exactions. Because within himself he knows that she is everything and all things for the life and joy of men, therefore he would seem perfect in her eyes; and he rails against whatsoever in her does not please him, as a blot upon the lustre of his ideal, which indeed he would make a glorified reflexion of his own faults. When he is most imperfect, he most exacts her praise; when he is weakest, she must think him most strong; when he fails, she must call failure victory, or at the least she must name it honourable defeat; she must not see his meanness, but she must magnify the smallest of his generosities to the great measure of his immeasurable vanity therein; she must see faith in his unfaithfulness, honour in his disgrace, heroism in his cowardice, for his sake; she must forgive freely and forgettingly such injury as he would not pardon any man;

in one word, she must love him, that in her love he may think and boast himself a god.

It is much to ask. And yet many a woman who loves a man with all her heart has done and daily does every one of those things, and more; and the man knows it, and will not think of it lest he should die of shame. And, moreover, a woman has borne him, a woman has nursed him, a woman taught him first; a woman gives him her soul and her body when he is a man; and when he is dead, if tears are shed for him, they are a woman's.

If we men are honest, we shall say that we do not give her much for all that, not much honour, not much faith. We think we do enough if we give her life's necessities and luxuries in fair share to the limit of our poverty or wealth; that we give much, if we love her; too much, if we trust her altogether.

It is a wonder that women should love, seeing what some men are and what most men may be when the devil is in them. It is a wonder that women should not rise up in a body and demand laws to free them from marriage, for one-half the cause that so many of them have.

But they do not. Even in this old age of history they still believe in marriage, and cling to it, and in vast majority cry out against its dissolution. No man ever believes in anything as a woman who loves him believes in him. Men have stronger arms, and heads for harder work, but they have no such hearts as women. And the world has been led by the heart in all ages.

Even when the great mistake is made, many a woman clings to the faith that made it, for the sake of what might have been, in a self-respect of which men do not dream. Even when she has married with little love, and taken a man who has turned upon her like a brute beast, her marriage is still a bond which she will not break, and the vow made is not void because the promise taken has been a vain lie. Its damnation is upon him who spoke it, but she still keeps faith.

So, when her fair years of youth lay scattered and withered as blown leaves along the desert of her past, Helen Harmon, wisely or unwisely, but faithfully and with a whole heart, meant to keep that plighted word which is not to be broken by wedded man and woman 'until death shall them part.'

CHAPTER V

Miss Wimpole was walking up and down the little sitting-room in considerable perplexity. When she was greatly in doubt as to her future conduct, she puckered her elderly lips, frowned severely, and talked to herself with an occasional energetic shaking of the head. She always did up her hair very securely and neatly, so that this was quite safe. Women who are not sure of their hairpins carry their heads as carefully as a basket of eggs and do not bend them if they have to stoop for anything.

Talking to oneself is a bad habit, especially when the door is open, whether one be swearing at something or examining one's own conscience. But Miss Wimpole could not help it, and the question of returning the price of the hat to Archie Harmon's mother was such a very difficult one, that she had forgotten to shut the door.

"Most impossible situation!" she repeated aloud. "Most terrible situation! Poor boy! Half idiotic — father mad. Most distressing situation! If I tell his mother, I shall hurt her feelings dreadfully. If I tell Richard, I shall hurt his feelings dreadfully. If I tell nobody, I shall break my promise to Sylvia, besides putting her in the position of accepting a hat from a young man. Ridiculous present, a hat! If it had only been a parasol! Parasols are not so ridiculous as hats. I wonder why! Perfectly impossible to keep the money, of course. Even Judas Iscariot — dear me! Where are my thoughts running to? Shocking! But a terrible situation. It was dear, too — eighty francs! We must get it into Mrs. Harmon's hands somehow — "

"Why must you get eighty francs into Mrs. Harmon's hands?" enquired the colonel, laying his hat upon a chair.

The door had been open, and he had heard her talking while he was in the corridor. She uttered an exclamation as she turned and saw him.

"Oh — well — I suppose you heard me. I must really cure myself of talking when I am alone! But I was not saying anything in particular."

"You were saying that you must manage to pay Mrs. Harmon eighty francs. It is very easy, for she happens to be here and I have just seen her."

"Oh, I know she is here!" cried Miss Wimpole. "I know it to my cost! She and that — and her son, you know."

"Yes, I know. But what is the matter? What is the trouble?"

"Oh, Richard! You are so sensitive about anything that has to do with Mrs. Harmon!"

"I?" The colonel looked at her quietly.

"Yes. Of course you are, and it is quite natural and I quite understand, and I do not blame you in the least. But such a dreadful thing has happened. I hardly know how I can tell you about it. It is really too dreadful for words."

Wimpole sat down and fanned himself slowly with the Paris *Herald*. He was still rather pale, for his nerves had been shaken.

"Rachel, my dear," he said mildly, "don't be silly. Tell me what is the matter."

Miss Wimpole walked slowly once round the room, stopped at the window and looked through the blinds, and at last turned and faced her brother with all the energy of her seasoned character.

"Richard," she began, "don't call me silly till you hear. It's awful. That boy suddenly appeared in a shop where Sylvia was buying a hat, and paid for it and vanished."

"Eh? What's that?" asked Wimpole, opening his eyes wide. "I don't think I quite understood, Rachel. I must have been thinking of something else, just then."

"I daresay you were," replied his sister, severely. "You are growing dreadfully absent-minded. You really should correct it. I say that when Sylvia was buying a hat, just now, Archie Harmon suddenly appeared in the shop and spoke to us. Then he asked Sylvia whether she liked the hat she was trying on, and she said she did. Then he went off, and when we wished to pay we were told that the hat had been paid for by the young gentleman. Now —"

The colonel interrupted and startled his sister by laughing aloud at this point. He could not help it, though he had not felt in the least as though he could laugh at anything for a long time, when he had entered the room. Miss Wimpole was annoyed.

"Richard," she said solemnly, "you surprise me."

"Does it not strike you as funny?" asked the colonel, recovering.

"No. It is — it is almost tragic. But perhaps," she continued, with a fine point of irony, "since you make so light of the matter, you will be good enough to return to Mrs. Harmon the price of the hat purchased by her half-witted boy for your ward."

"Don't call him half-witted, Rachel," said the colonel. "It's not so bad as that, you know."

"I cannot agree with you," replied his sister. "Only an idiot would think of rushing into a shop where a lady is buying something, and suddenly paying for it. You must admit that, Richard. Only an idiot could do such a thing."

"I have done just such a thing myself," observed Wimpole, thoughtfully, for he remembered the miniature he had bought for Helen that afternoon. "I suppose I was an idiot, since you say —"

"I said nothing of the kind, my dear! How can you accuse me of calling you an idiot? Really, Richard, you behave very strangely to-day! I don't know what can be the matter with you. First, you manage to make Sylvia cry her eyes out — Heaven knows what dreadful thing you said to her! And now you deliberately accuse me of calling you an idiot. If this sort of thing goes on much longer, there will be an end of our family happiness."

"This is not one of my lucky days," said the colonel, resignedly, and he laid down the folded newspaper. "How much did the hat cost? I will return the money to Mrs. Harmon, and explain."

Miss Wimpole looked at him with gratitude and admiration in her face.

"It was eighty francs," she answered. "Richard, I did not call you an idiot. In the first place, it would have been totally untrue, and in the second place, it would have been — what shall I say? It would have been very vulgar to call you an idiot, Richard. It is a vulgar expression."

"It might have been true, my dear, but I certainly never knew you to say anything vulgar. On the other hand, I really did not assert that you applied the epithet to me. I applied it to myself, rather experimentally. And poor Archie Harmon is not so bad as that, either."

"If he is not idiotic — or — or something like it, why do you say 'poor' Archie?"

"Because I am sorry for him," returned the colonel. "And so are you," he added presently.

Miss Wimpole considered the matter for a few seconds; then she slowly nodded, and came up to him.

"I am," she said. "Richard, kiss me."

That was always the proclamation of peace, not after strife, for they never quarrelled, but at the close of an argument. It was done in this way. The colonel rose, and stood before his sister; then both bent their heads a little, and as their cool grey cheeks touched, each kissed the air somewhere in the neighbourhood of the other's ear. They had been little children together, and their mother had taught them to 'kiss and make friends,' as good children should, whenever there had been any difference; and now they were growing old together, but they had never forgotten, in nearly fifty years, to 'kiss and make friends' when they had disagreed. What is childlike is not always childish.

The colonel resumed his seat, and there was silence for a few minutes. The folded newspaper lay on the table unread, and he looked at it, scarcely aware that he saw it.

"I think Archie Harmon must have fallen in love with Sylvia," he said at last. "That is the only possible explanation. She has grown up since he saw her last, and so has he, though his mind has not developed much, I suppose."

"Not at all, I should say," answered Miss Wimpole. "But I wish you would not suggest such things. The mere idea makes me uncomfortable."

"Yes," assented the colonel, thoughtfully. "We will not talk about it."

Suddenly he knew what he was looking at, and he read the first head-lines on the paper, just visible above the folded edge. The words were 'Harmon Sane,' printed in large capitals. In a moment he had spread out the sheet.

The big letters only referred to a short telegram, lower down. "It is reported on good authority that Henry Harmon, who has been an inmate of the Bloomingdale Insane Asylum for some years, is recovering rapidly, and will shortly be able to return to his numerous friends in perfect mental health."

That was all. The colonel searched the paper from beginning to end, in the vain hope of finding something more, and read the little paragraph over and over again. There was no possibility of a mistake. There had never been but one Henry Harmon, and there could certainly be but one in the Bloomingdale asylum. The news was so sudden that Wimpole felt his heart stand still when he first read it, and as he thought of it he grew cold, and shivered as though he had an ague.

It had been easier to think of Harmon's possible recovery before he had seen that scar on Helen's forehead. For many years he had borne the thought that the woman he had silently loved so long was bound to a man little better than a beast; but it had never occurred to him that she might have had much to bear of which he had known nothing, even to violence and physical danger. The knowledge had changed him within the last hour, and the news about Harmon now hardened him all at once in his anger, as hot steel is chilled when it has just reached the cutting temper, and does not change after that.

The colonel was as honourable a man as ever shielded a woman's good name, or rode to meet an enemy in fair fight. He was chivalrous with all the world, and quixotic with himself. He had charity for the ways of other men, for he had seen enough to know that many things were done by men whom no one would dare to call dishonourable, which he would not have done to save his own life. He understood that such a lasting love as his was stronger than himself, yet he himself had been so strong that he had never yielded even to its thoughts, nor ever allowed the longing for a final union with Helen at all costs to steal upon his unguarded imagination.

He was not tempted beyond his strength, indeed, and in his apparent perfection, that must be remembered. In all those years of his devoted friendship Helen had never let him guess that she could have loved him once, much less that she loved him now, as he did her, with the same resolution to hide from her inward eyes what she could not tear from her inmost heart. But it is never fair to say that if a man had been placed in a certain imaginary position, he might have been weak. So long as he has not broken down under the trials and burdens of real life, he has a right to be called strong.

The colonel set no barrier, however, against the devotion to Helen's welfare which he might honourably feel and show. In day-dreams over old books he had envied those clean knights of a younger time, who fought for wives not theirs so openly and bravely, and so honestly that the spotless women for whom they faced death took lustre of more honour from such unselfish love. And for Helen's sake he had longed for some true circumstance of mortal danger in which to prove once more how well and silently an honest man can die to save an innocent woman.

But those were dreams. In acts he had done much, though never half of what he had always wished to do. The trouble had all come little by little in Helen's existence, and there had not been one great deciding moment in which his hand or head could have saved her happiness.

Now it seemed as though the time were full, and as if he might at last, by one deed, cast the balance by the scale of happiness. He did not know how to do it, nor whither to turn, but he felt, as he sat by the table with the little newspaper in his hand, that unless he could prevent Harmon from coming back to his wife, his own existence was to turn out a miserable failure, his love a lie, and his long devotion but a worthless word.

His first impulse was to leave Lucerne that

night and reach home in the shortest possible time. He would see Harmon and tell him what he thought, and force from him a promise to leave Helen in peace, some unbreakable promise which the man should not be able to deny, some sort of bond that should have weight in law.

The colonel's nostrils quivered, and his steady grey eyes fixed themselves and turned very light as he thought of the interview and of the quiet, hard words he would select. Each one of them should be a retribution in itself. He was the gentlest of men, but under great provocation he could be relentless.

What would Harmon answer? The colonel grew thoughtful again. Harmon would ask him, with an intonation that would be an insult to Helen, what right Wimpole had acquired to take Helen's part against him, her lawful husband. It would be hard to answer that, having no right of his own to fight her battles, least of all against the man she had married.

He might answer by reminding Harmon of old times. He might say that he at least resigned the hope of that right, when Harmon had been his friend, because he had believed that it was for Helen's happiness.

That would be but a miserably unsatisfactory answer, though it would be the truth. The colonel did not remember that he had ever wished to strike a man with a whip until the present moment. But the sight of the cut on Helen's forehead had changed him very quickly. He was not sure that he could keep his hands from Harmon if he should see him. And slowly a sort of cold and wrathful glow rose in his face, and he felt as though his long, thin fingers were turning into steel springs.

Miss Wimpole had taken up a book and was reading. She heard him move in his chair, and looked up and saw his expression.

"What is the matter with you, Richard?" she enquired, in surprise.

"Why?" He started nervously.

"You look like the destroying angel," she observed calmly. "I suppose you are gradually beginning to be angry about Sylvia's hat, as I was. I don't wonder."

"Oh yes — Sylvia's hat; yes, yes, I remember." The colonel passed his hand over his eyes. "I mean, it is perhaps the heat. It's a warm day. I'll go to my room for a while."

"Yes, do, my dear. You behave so strangely to-day — as if you were going to be ill."

But the colonel was already gone, and was stalking down the corridor with his head high, his eyes as hard as polished grey stones, and his nervous hands clenched as they swung a little with his gait.

His sister shook her head energetically, then slowly and sadly, as she watched him in the distance.

"How much more gracefully we grow old than men!" she said aloud, and took up her book again.

CHAPTER VI

HELEN had not seen the paragraph about Harmon. She rarely read newspapers, and generally trusted to other people to learn what they contained. The majority read papers for amusement, or for the sort of excitement produced on nervous minds by short, strong shocks often repeated. There are persons who ponder the paper daily for half an hour in absorbed silence, and then lift up their voices and cackle out all they have read, as a hen runs about and cackles when she has laid an egg. They fly at every one they see, an unnatural excitement in every tone and gesture, and ask in turn whether each friend has heard that this one is engaged to be married, and that another is dead and has left all his money to a hospital. When they have asked all the questions they can think of, without waiting for an answer, they relapse into their normal condition, and become again as other men and women are. Very few really read the papers in order to follow the course of events for the mere sake of information. Mrs.

Harmon was more or less indifferent to things that neither directly concerned her nor appealed to her tastes and sympathies.

Her letters were brought to her before she had left the sitting-room after the colonel had gone away, and she looked at the addresses on them carelessly, passing them from one hand to the other as one passes cards. One arrested her attention, among the half-dozen or so which she had received. It was the regular report from the asylum, posted on the first of the month. But it was thicker than usual; and when she tore open the envelope, rather nervously and with a sudden anticipation of trouble, a second sealed letter dropped from the single folded sheet contained in the first. But even that one sheet was full, instead of bearing only the few lines she always received to tell her that there was no change in her husband's condition.

There had been a change, and a great one. Since last writing, said the doctor, Harmon had suddenly begun to improve. At first he had merely seemed more quiet and patient than formerly; then, in the course of a few days, he had begun to ask intelligent questions, and had clearly understood that he had been insane for some time and was still in an asylum. He had rapidly learned the names of the people about him, and had not afterwards confused them, but remembered them with remarkable accuracy. Day by day he had improved, and was still improving. He had enquired about the state of his affairs, and had wished to see one or two of his old friends. More than once he had asked after his wife, and had evidently been glad to hear that she was well. Then he had written a letter to her, which the doctor immediately forwarded. So far as it was possible to form a judgment in the case, the improvement seemed to promise permanent recovery; though no one could tell, of course, whether a return to the world might not mean also a return to the unfortunate habit which had originally unbalanced Harmon's mind, but from which he was safe as long as he remained where he was.

It was not easy for Helen to read to the end of such a letter: it shook in her hands as she went on from one sentence to the next, and the sealed envelope slipped from her knees to the floor while she was reading. When she had got to the end, she stared a moment at the signature, and then folded the sheet, almost unconsciously, and drew her nail sharply along the folds, as though she would make the paper feel what she felt, and suffer as she suffered, in every nerve of her body, and in every secret fibre of her soul.

She had not believed a recovery possible. Now that it was a fact, she knew how utterly beyond probability she had thought it; and immediately the great problem rose before her, confusing, vast, terrifying. But before she faced it she must read Harmon's letter.

It had fallen to the floor, and she had to look for it and find it and pick it up. The handwriting was large, somewhat ornamental, yet heavy in parts and not always regular. As she glanced at the address, she remembered how she had disliked the writing when she had first seen it, at a time when she had seen much to admire in Harmon himself. Now she did not like to touch the envelope on which he had written her name, and she unreasoningly feared the contact of the sheet it held, as of something that might defile her and must surely hurt her cruelly. The hand that had traced the characters on the paper was the hand that had struck her and left its mark for all her life. And as she remembered the rest, an enormous loathing of the man who was still her husband took possession of her, so that she could not open the letter for a few moments.

It was at once a loathing of bodily disgust, like a sickness, and a mental horror of a creature who was so far from her natural nobility that it frightened her to know how she hated him, and she began to fear the letter itself, lest it should make some great change in her for which she should at last hate herself also. The spasm ran all through her, as the sight of some very disgusting evil thing violently disturbs body and mind at the same time.

The temptation to destroy the letter unread came upon her with all possible force, and the vision of a return to peace was before her eyes, as though the writing were already burned and beyond her power to recover. But that would be cowardly, and she was brave. With drawn lips, pale cheeks, and knitted brows she opened it, took out the folded contents, and began to read. As though to remind her of the place where he was, and of all the circumstances from first to last, the name of the asylum was printed at the head of each sheet in small, businesslike letters.

She began to read:

My Dear Helen,— You will be surprised to hear directly from me, I suppose, and I can hardly expect that you will be pleased, though you are too good not to be glad that I am better after my long illness. I have a great many things to write to you, and no particular right to hope that you will read them. Will you? I hope so, for I do not mean to write again until I get an answer to this letter. But if you do read this one, please believe that I am quite in my right senses again, and that I mean all I say. Besides, the doctor has written to you. He considers me almost 'safe' now. I mean, safe to remain as I am.

It is not easy for me to write to you. You must hate me, of course. God knows, I have given you reason enough to wish that I might stay here for the rest of my life. You are a very good woman, and perhaps you will forgive me for all I have done to hurt you. That is the main thing I wanted to say. I want to ask your pardon and forgiveness for everything, from beginning to end.

'Everything' is a big word, I know. There has been a great deal during these many years,—a great deal more than I like to think of; for the more I think of it, the less I see how you can forgive even the half, much less forget it.

I was not myself, Helen. You have a right to say that it was my fault if I was not myself. I drank hard. That is not an excuse, I know; but it was the cause of most of the things I did. No woman can ever understand how a man feels who drinks, and has got so far that he cannot give it up. How should she? But you know that most men cannot give it up, and that it is a sort of disease, and can be treated scientifically. But I do not mean to make excuses. I only ask your forgiveness, and in order to forgive me you will find better excuses for me than I could invent for myself. I throw myself upon your kindness, for that is the only thing I can do.

They say that it would not be quite safe for me to leave the asylum for another month or two, and I am quite resigned to that; for the life is quiet here, and I feel quiet myself and hate the idea of excitement. I suppose I have had too much of it.

But by and by they will insist upon my leaving, when I am considered quite cured; and then I want to go back to you, and try to make you happy, and do my best to make up to you for all the harm I have done you.

Perhaps you think it is impossible, but I am very much changed since you saw me.

I know what I am asking, dear Helen. Do not think I ask it as though it were a mere trifle. But I know what you are and what you have done. You could have got a divorce over and over again, and I believe you could now if you liked. It is pretty easy in some states, and I suppose I could not find much to say in defence. Yet you have not done it. I do not know whether you have ever thought of it.

If you think of it now that I want to come back to you and try to do better, and make you happy, for God's sake give me another chance before you take any step. Give me one more chance, Helen, for the sake of old times. You used to like me once, and we were very happy at first. Then — well, it was all my fault, it was every bit of it my fault, and I would give my soul to undo it. If you will forgive me, we can try together and begin over again, and it shall all be different, for I will be different.

Can we not try? Will you try? It will be easy if you will only let us begin. It is not as if we should have other troubles to deal with, for we have plenty of friends and plenty of money, and I will do the rest. I solemnly promise that I will, if you will forgive me and begin over again. I know it must seem almost impossible. It would be quite impossible for any other woman, though you can do it if you will.

I shall wait for your answer, before I write again, though it will seem a very long time, and I am very anxious about it. If it is what I hope it will be, perhaps you will cable a few words, even one word. 'Forgiven' is only one word. Will you not say it? Will you not give me one chance more? Oh, Helen dear, for God's sake, do! H.

Helen read the letter to the end, through every phrase and every repetition. Then the fight began, and it was long and bitter, a battle to death, of which she could not see the issue.

The man wrote in earnest, and sincerely meant what he said. No one could read the words and doubt that. Helen believed all he had written, so far as his intention was concerned, but she could not cut his life in two and leave out of the question the man he had been, in order to receive without fear or disgust the man he professed himself to be. That was too much to ask of any woman who had suffered what she had of neglect, of violence, of shame.

'No one could tell,' the doctor wrote, 'whether a return to the world might not mean also a return to the unfortunate habit' — no one could tell that. And Harmon himself wrote that most men could not give it up, that it was a disease, and that no woman could understand it. What possible surety could he give that it should never get hold of him again? None. But that was only a small matter in the whole question.

If she had ever loved him, perhaps if she could have felt that he had ever loved her truly, it would have been different. But she could not. Why had he married her? For her beauty. The shame of it rose in her eyes as she sat alone, and she could not help turning her face from the light.

For love's sake, even for an old love, outraged long ago and scarred past recognizing, she could have forgiven much. Old memories, suddenly touched, are always more tender than we have thought they were, till the tears rise for them, and the roots of the old life stir in the heart.

Helen had nothing of that. She had made the great mistake of marrying a man whom she had not loved, but whom she had admired, and perhaps believed in, more than she understood. She had married him because he seemed to love her very much, and the thought of being so loved was pleasant. She had soon found out what such love meant, and by and by she had seen how traces of it survived in Henry Harmon, when all thought of honouring her, or even of respecting her, was utterly gone.

A bitter laugh rang through the quiet room, and she started, for it was her own voice. She was to forgive! Did he know what he was asking, and for what things he was praying forgiveness? Yet when he was sober he had generally remembered what he had done when he had been drunk. That is to say, he had seemed to have the faculty of remembering what he chose to recall, and of forgetting everything else. She was to forgive what he chose to remember!

'Oh, Helen dear, for God's sake, do!' She could see the last written words of his letter before her eyes, though the sheet was folded and bent double in her tightly closed hand. He meant it, and it was an appeal for mercy. She hated herself for having laughed so cruelly a moment earlier. There was a cry in the words, quite different from all he had written before them. It did not touch her, it hardly appealed to her at all, but somehow it gave him the right to be heard, for it was human.

Then she went over all he said, though it hurt her. She was not a woman of quick impulses, and she knew that what was left of her life was in the balance. Even he seemed to acknowledge that, for he spoke of a possibility of freedom for her by divorce. To speak so easily of it, he must have thought of it often, and that meant that it was really an easy matter, as Colonel Wimpole had said. It was in her power, and she had free will. He knew that she had a choice, and that she could either take him back, now that he was cured, or make it utterly out of the question for him to approach her. He said as much, when he implored her to give him one more chance 'before taking any step.' She went over and over it all, for hours.

In the cool of the evening she opened the blinds, collected her letters, and then sat down again, no nearer to a decision than she had been at first. A servant came and told her that Colonel Wimpole was downstairs. He had written a word on his card, asking to see her again.

Her first impulse was the natural one. She would let him come in and she would lay the whole matter before him, as before the best friend she had in the world, and ask him how she should act. There was not in all the world a man more honourable and just. She would let him come to her.

The words were on her lips, while the servant stood in the open door, waiting for her answer. She checked herself with an effort. She wrote a line and gave it to the man.

She would not see Wimpole just then, for it would not be fair to him nor perhaps quite just to Harmon. Wimpole loved her, though he was quite unaware that she knew it. She believed firmly that when he had advised her that very afternoon to divorce her husband, he was thinking only of her happiness; but he had advised it, all the same, just because he believed that Harmon might recover. He could not change his mind now that what he feared for her was taking place. How could he? He would use every argument in his power, and he would find many good ones, against her returning to her husband. He could influence her against her free will, and far more than he could guess, because she loved him secretly as much as he loved her. It was bitter not to see him, and tell him, and ask his help; it was desperately hard, but as soon as she saw that it was right, she wrote the words that must send him away, before she could have time to hesitate. Deep in her heart, too, there was a thought for him. Loving her as he did, it would not be easy for him, either, to go into the whole matter. His honour and his love would have to fight it out. So she sent him away.

Then Archie came into the room, vague and childish at first, but with an odd look in his eyes, and he began to talk to her about Sylvia Strahan in a way that frightened her, little by little, as he went on.

"Marry me to her, mother," he said at last, as though asking for the simplest thing. "I want to be married, and I want Sylvia. I never saw any other girl whom I wanted."

CHAPTER VII

THERE are times when trouble accumulates as an avalanche, or like water in one of those natural intermittent springs that break out plentifully, and dry up altogether in a sort of alternation. But the spring has its regular period, and trouble has not, and in an avalanche of disasters it is impossible to say at any moment whether the big boulders have all passed in the sliding drift of smaller stuff, or whether the biggest of all may not be yet coming.

There are days in a lifetime which decide all the rest, and sometimes explain all that has gone before, happy days, or days of tears, as the case may be. Perhaps they are the most interesting days to describe, after all, for they are the ones which generally terminate a period in existence. But many say that in real life situations, as they are called, never have any satisfactory termination, and that the story which is most true of men and women is that one which has neither beginning nor end. The fact is that what appears to be the beginning is often in reality the termination of a long series of events. Novels often end in marriage, yet real life frequently begins there. There is a very old proverb to that effect.

On such days all sorts of things happen that never occurred before and perhaps never occur again, and every one who has had one or two such short and eventful periods of confusion can remember how a host of unforeseen trifles thrust themselves forward to disturb him. It was as though nothing could turn out right, as if nobody could take a message without a mistake, as if the post and the telegraph had conspired together to send letters and telegrams to wrong addresses, and altogether all things, including the most sober and reliable institutions, seem to work backwards against results instead of for them. Those are bad times. When they last long, people come to grief. When they are soon over, people laugh at them. When they decide a whole life, as they sometimes do, people can afterwards trace the causes of happiness or disaster to some very small lucky coincidence or unfortunate mistake over which they themselves had no control.

When Colonel Wimpole had left Helen so abruptly, he had looked upon his going away as a mere interruption of his visit, necessary, because he could not be sure of controlling himself just then, but not meant to last any length of time. But after so suddenly learning the change in Harmon's condition, he would have waited till the evening before going back, if his sister had not been so absurdly nervous about the price of the hat, insisting that he should go at once and return the money. He had gone to his own room in a disturbed state of mind and had stayed there an hour, after which Miss Wimpole, judging that he must be sufficiently rested, had knocked at his door and urged him to go at once to see Mrs. Harmon. As he had no very good reason to give for refusing to do so, he had made the attempt and had been refused admittance. He went for a walk along the lake and came back again after an hour, and wrote on his card a special request.

"May I see you now? It is about a rather awkward little matter."

It was growing late. Helen reflected that he could not stay long before his own dinner time and hers, that he evidently had something especial to say, and that she was certainly strong enough to keep her own counsel for a quarter of an hour if she made up her mind to do so. Besides, it must seem strange to him to be refused a second time; he would infer that something was wrong and would ask questions when they next met. She decided to see him.

His face was grave, and he was quite calm again. As he took her hand and spoke, there was a sort of quiet tenderness in his manner and tone, a little beyond what he usually showed, perceptible to her, who longed for it, though it could hardly have been noticed by any one else.

"It is rather an awkward little matter," he said, repeating the words he had written.

Then he saw her face in the twilight, and he guessed that she had seen the newspaper.

"You are in trouble," he said quickly.

She hesitated and turned from him, for she had forgotten that her face must betray her distress.

"Yes," she answered, but she said no more than that.

"Can I help you?" he asked after a short pause.

"Please do not ask me."

She sat down, and Wimpole sighed audibly as he took his seat at a little distance from her. He knew that she must have seen the paragraph about Harmon's recovery.

"Then I will explain my errand," he said. "May I?"

It seemed rather a relief to have so small a matter ready to hand.

"Yes. It will not take long, will it?" she

asked rather nervously, for she felt how his presence tempted her to confidence. "It — it will soon be dinner time, you know."

"I shall not stay long," said the colonel, quietly. "It is rather an awkward little matter. You know Archie was with you this morning when I saw you in the shop and got that miniature."

Helen looked at him suddenly with a change of expression, expecting some new trouble.

"Yes, Archie was with us. What is it?" Her voice was full of a new anxiety.

"It is nothing of any great importance," answered Wimpole, quickly, for he saw that she was nervous. "Only, he went out by himself afterwards, and came across my sister and Sylvia in a milliner's shop — "

"What was he doing in a milliner's shop?" interrupted Helen, in surprise.

"I don't know," said the colonel. "I fancy he saw them through the window and went in to speak to them. Sylvia was trying on a hat, you know, and she liked it, and Archie, without saying anything, out of pure goodness of heart, I suppose — "

He hesitated. On any other day he would have smiled, but just now he was as deeply disturbed as Helen herself, and the absurd incident of the hat assumed a tremendous importance.

"Well? What did he do?" Helen's nerves were on edge, and she spoke almost sharply.

"He paid for the hat," answered Wimpole, with an air of profound sorrow, and even penitence, as if it had been all his fault. "And then he went off, before they knew it."

Helen bit her lip, for it trembled. He had not told the story very clearly or connectedly, but she understood. Archie had just been talking to her strangely about Sylvia, and she had seen that he had fallen in love with his old playmate, and she was afraid. And now, she was horribly ashamed for him. It was so stupid, so pitifully stupid.

The colonel, guessing what greater torment was tearing at her heart, sat still in a rather dejected attitude, waiting for her to speak, but not watching her.

The matter which had brought him was certainly not very terrible in itself, but it stirred and quickened all the ever-growing pain for her son which was a part of her daily life. It knitted its strength to that of all the rest, to hurt her cruelly, and the torture was more than she could bear.

She turned suddenly in her seat and half buried her face against the back of the chair, so that Wimpole could not see it, and she bit the coarse velvet savagely, trying to be silent and tearless till he should go away. But he knew what she was doing. If he had not spoken, she could still have kept back the scalding tears awhile. But he did speak, and very gently.

"Helen — dear Helen — what is it?"

"My heart is breaking," she said, almost quietly.

But then the tears came, and she shook once or twice, like an animal that has a deep wound but cannot die. The tears came slowly, and burned her like drops of fire. She kept her face turned away.

Wimpole was beside her and held her passive hand. It twitched painfully as it lay in his, and every agonized movement of it shot through him, but he could not say anything at first. Besides, she knew he was there and would help her if he could. At last he spoke his thought.

"I will keep him from you," he said. "He shall not come near you."

Her hand tightened upon his, instantly, and she sat up in her chair, turning her face to him, quite white in the dusk, by the open window.

"Then you know?" she asked.

"Yes. It is in the Paris paper to-day. But it is only a report. I do not believe it is true."

She rose, mastering herself, as she withdrew her hand, and steadied herself a moment against the chair beside him.

"It is true," she said. "He has recovered. He has written to me."

Wimpole felt as if he had been condemned to death without warning.

"When?" he managed to ask.

"I got the letter this afternoon."

Their voices answered each other, dull and colourless in the gloom, and for some moments neither spoke. Helen went to the window and leaned upon the broad marble sill, breathing the evening air from the lake, and Wimpole followed her. The electric lamps were lighted in the street, glaring coldly out of the grey dusk, and many people were moving slowly along the pavement below, in little parties, some gay, some silent.

"That is why I did not let you come up," said Helen, after a long time. "But now — since you know —" She stopped, still hesitating, and he tried to see her expression, but there was not enough light.

"Yes?" he said, with a question, not pressing her, but waiting.

"Since you know," she answered at last, "you can guess the rest."

A spasm of pain half choked her, and Wimpole put out his hand to lay it gently upon her arm, but drew it back again. He had never done even that much in all those years, and he would not do it now.

"I will keep him from you," he said again.

"No. You must not do that." Her voice was steady again. "He will not come to me against my will."

Wimpole turned sharply as he leaned on the window-sill beside her, for he did not understand.

"You cannot possibly be thinking of writing to him, of letting him come back?"

"Yes," she said. "That is what I am thinking of doing."

She hardly dared think that she still could hesitate, now that Wimpole was beside her. If he had not come, it might have been different. But he was close to her now, and she knew how long and well he had loved her. Alone, she could have found reasons for refusing ever to see Harmon again, but they lost their look of honour now that this man, who was everything to her, was standing at her elbow. Exaggerating her danger, she feared lest Wimpole should influence her, even unintentionally, if she left the question open. And he, for her own happiness and honourably setting all thoughts of himself aside, believed that he ought to use whatever influence he had, to the utmost.

"You must not do it," he said. "I implore you not to think of it. You will wreck your life."

She did not move, for she had known what he would say.

"If you are my friend," she answered, after a pause, "you should wish me to do what is right."

It was a trite commonplace, but she never tried to be original, at any time, and just then the words exactly expressed her thought. He resented it.

"You have done more than enough of that sort of right already. It is time you thought a little of yourself. I do not mean only of your happiness, but of your safety. You are not safe with that man. He will drink again, and he may kill you."

She turned her white face deliberately towards him in the gloom.

"And do you think I am afraid of that?" she asked slowly.

There was a sort of reproach in the tone, and a great good pride with it. Wimpole did not know what to say, and merely bent his head gravely.

"Besides," she added, "he is in earnest. He is sorry. He was mad then, and he asks me to forgive him now. How can I refuse? He was really mad, really insane. No one can deny it. Shall I?"

"You can forgive him without going back to him. Why should you risk your life?"

"It is the only way of showing him that I forgive him, and my life will not be in danger."

"Do you think that you can ever be happy again, if you go back to him?" asked Wimpole.

"My happiness is not the question. The only thing that matters is to do right."

"It seems to me that right is more or less dependent on its results—"

"Never!" cried Helen, almost fiercely, and drawing back a little against the side of the window. "If one syllable of that were true, then we could never know whether we were doing right or not, till we could judge the result. And the end would justify the means, always, and there would be no more right and wrong at all in the world."

"But when you know the results?" objected Wimpole. "It seems to me that it may be different."

"Then it is fear! Then one is afraid to do right because one knows that one risks being hurt! What sort of morality would that be? It would be contemptible."

"But suppose that it is not only yourself who may be hurt, but some one else? One should think of others first. That is right, too." He could not help saying that much.

Helen hesitated a moment.

"Yes," she answered presently. "But no one else is concerned in this case."

"I will leave your friends out of the question," said Wimpole. "Do you think it will do Archie any good to live under the same roof with his father?"

Helen started perceptibly.

"Oh, why did you say that!" she exclaimed in a low voice, and as she leaned over the window-sill again she clasped her hands together in a sort of despairing way. "Why did you say that!" she repeated.

Wimpole was silent, for he had not at first realized that he had found a very strong argument. As yet, being human, she had thought only of herself, in the first hours of her trouble. He had recalled all her past terrors for her unfortunate son, and the memory of all she had done to keep him out of his father's way in old days. He had been a mere boy, then, and it had been just possible, because his half-developed mind was not suspicious. Now that he was grown up, it would be another matter. The prospect was hideous enough, if Harmon should take a fancy to the young man, and make him his companion, and then fall back into his old ways.

"Why did you say it? Why did you make me think of that?" Helen asked the questions almost piteously. "I should have to send Archie away — somewhere, where he would be safe."

"How could he be safe without you?" The argument was pitilessly just.

But, after all, her life and happiness were at stake. Wimpole saw right in everything that could withhold her from the step to which she had evidently made up her mind.

"And if I refuse to go back to my husband, what will become of him?" she asked, still clasping her hands hard together.

"He could be properly taken care of," suggested Wimpole.

"And would that be forgiveness?" Helen turned to him again energetically.

"It would be wisdom, at all events."

"Ah, now you come back to your argument!" Her voice changed. "You are pressing me to do what is wise, not what is right. Don't do that! Please don't do that!"

"Do you forgive him?" asked the colonel, very gravely.

Again she paused before answering him.

"Why should you doubt it?" she asked in her turn. "Don't you see that I wish to go back to him?"

"You know what I mean. It is not the same thing. You are a very good woman, and by sheer force of goodness you could make an enormous sacrifice for the sake of what you thought right."

"And would not that be forgiveness?"

"No. If you freely forgave him, it would be no sacrifice, for you would believe in him again. You would have just the same faith in Harmon which you had on the day you married him. If forgiveness means anything, it means that one takes back the man who has hurt one, on the same real, inward terms with oneself on which one formerly lived with him. You cannot do that, for it would not be sane."

"No, I cannot quite do that," Helen answered, after a moment's thought. "It would not be true to say that I had even thought I could. But then, if you put it in that way, it would be hard to forgive any one, and it would generally be foolish. There is something wrong about your way of looking at it."

"I am not a woman," said Wimpole, simply. "That is what is the matter. At the same time, I do not see how you, as a woman, are ever going to reconcile what you believe to be your duty to Harmon with what is certainly your duty to your son."

"I must," said Helen. "I must."

"Then you must do it before you write to Harmon, for afterwards it will be impossible. You must decide first what you will do with

Archie to keep him out of danger. When you have made up your mind about that, if you choose to sacrifice yourself, nobody can prevent you. At least you will not be ruining him, too."

He saw no reason for not putting the case plainly, since what he said was true. Yet as he felt his advantage, he knew that by pressing it he was increasing her perplexity. In all his life he had never been in so difficult a position. She stood close beside him, her arm almost touching his, and he had loved her all his life, as few men love, with an honesty and purity that were more than quixotic. What there was left, he could have borne for her sake, even to seeing her united again with Henry Harmon. But the thought of the risk she was running was more than he could bear. He would use argument, stratagem, force, anything, to keep her out of such a life; and when he had succeeded in saving her, he would be capable of denying himself even the sight of her, lest his conscience should accuse him of having acted for himself rather than for her alone.

He remembered Harmon's face as he had last seen it, coarse, cunning, seamed with dissipation, and he looked sideways at Helen, white, weary, bruised, a fast fading rose of yesterday, as she had called herself. The thought of Harmon's touch was more than he could bear.

"You shall not do it!" he exclaimed, after a long silence. "I will make it impossible."

Almost before he spoke the last words, he had repented them. Helen drew herself up and faced him, one hand on the window-sill.

"Colonel Wimpole," she said, "I know that you have always been my best friend. But you must not talk in that way. I cannot allow even you to come between me and what I think is right."

He bent his head a little.

"I beg your pardon," he answered, in a low voice. "I should have done it — not said it."

"I hope you will never think of it again," said Helen.

She left the window, and felt in the dark for matches, on the table, to light a small candle she used for sealing letters. It cast a faint light up to her sad face. Wimpole had stayed by the window, and watched her now, while she looked towards him over the little flame.

"Please go, now," she said gravely. "I cannot bear to talk about this any longer."

CHAPTER VIII

AFTER the door had closed, Helen stood a moment by the table, motionless. Then she sat down by the feeble light of the taper and wrote upon a sheet of paper her husband's address and one word — 'forgiven.' She looked at the writing fixedly for a minute or two, and then rang the bell.

"Have this telegram sent at once, please, and bring me a lamp and dinner," she said to the servant.

With the lamp came Archie, following it with a sort of interest, as children do.

"You must have been in the dark ever so long, mother," he said, and just then he saw her white face. "You are not looking all right," he observed.

Helen smiled, from force of habit, rather wearily. The servant began to set the table, moving stealthily, as though he were meditating some sudden surprise which never came. He was a fairly intelligent Swiss, with an immense pink face and very small blue eyes.

Helen watched him for a moment, and sighed. The man was intellectually her son's superior, and she knew it. Any one else might have smiled at the thought, as grotesque, but it had for her the cruel vividness of a misfortune that had saddened all of her life which her husband had not embittered. She envied, for her son, the poor waiter's little powers of mental arithmetic and memory.

"What's the matter, mother?" asked Archie, who sat looking at her.

"Nothing, dear," she answered, rousing herself, and smiling wearily again. "I am a little tired, perhaps. It has been a hot day."

"Has it? I didn't notice. I never do — at least, not much. I say, mother, let's go home! I'm tired of Europe, and I know you are. Let's all go home together — we and the Wimpoles."

"We shall be going home soon," said Helen.

"I thought you meant to go to Carlsbad first. Wasn't it to Carlsbad we were going?"

"Yes, dear. But — here comes dinner — we will talk about it by and by."

They sat down to table. In hotels abroad Helen always dined in her rooms, for she was never quite sure of Archie. He seemed strangely unconscious of his own defect of mind, and was always ready to enter boldly into conversation with his neighbours at a foreign hotel dinner table. His childish ignorance had once or twice caused her such humiliation as she did not feel called upon to bear again.

"I don't know why we shouldn't talk about it now," began Archie, when he had eaten his soup in silence, and the servant was changing his plate.

"We shall be alone, after dinner," answered his mother.

"Oh, the waiter doesn't care! He'll never see us again, you know, so why shouldn't we say anything we like before him?"

Mrs. Harmon looked at her son and shook her head gravely, which was an admonition he always understood.

"Did you see anything you liked, to-day?" she asked incautiously, by way of changing the conversation.

"Rather!" exclaimed Archie, promptly. "I met Sylvia Strahan — jukes!"

Helen shuddered, as she saw the look in his face and the glitter in his eyes.

"I wish you could remember not to say 'jukes' every other minute, Archie," she said, for the thousandth time.

"Do you think Sylvia minds when I say 'jukes'?" asked the young man, suddenly.

"I am sure she thinks it a very ugly and senseless word."

"Does she? Really?" He was silent for a few moments, pondering the question. "Well," he resumed at last, in a regretful tone, "I've always said it, and I like it, and I don't see any harm in it. But, of course, if Sylvia doesn't like it, I've got to give it up, that's all. I'm always going to do what Sylvia likes, now, as long as I live. And what you like, too, mother," he added as an apologetic and dutiful afterthought. "But then, you're pretty sure to like the same things, after all."

"You really must not go on in this way about Sylvia, my dear," said Helen. "It is too absurd."

Archie's heavy brows met right across his forehead as he looked up with something like a glare in his eyes, and his voice was suddenly thick and indistinct, when he answered.

"Don't call it absurd, mother. I don't understand what it is, but it's stronger than I am. I don't want anything but Sylvia. Things don't amuse me any more. It was only to-day—"

He stopped, for he was going to tell her how he had found no pleasure in his toys, neither in the blocks, nor in the tin soldiers, nor in the little papier-mâché lady and gentleman in the painted cart. But he thought she did not know about them, and he checked himself in a sudden shame which he had never felt before. A deep red blush spread over his dark face, and he looked down at his plate.

"I'm a man, now," he said, through his teeth, in a rough voice.

After that, he was silent for a time, but Helen watched him nervously. She, too, saw that he was a man, with almost less than a boy's mind, and her secret terror grew. She could not eat that evening, but he did not notice her. They dined quickly and then they sat down together, as they usually did, quite near to each other and side by side. She could sometimes teach him little things which he remembered, when everything was quiet. He generally began to talk of something he had seen, and she always tried to make him understand it and think about it. But this evening he said nothing for a long time, and she was glad of his silence. When she thought of the telegram she had sent, she had a sharp pain at her heart, and once or twice she started a little in her chair. But Archie did not notice her.

"I say, mother," he began, looking up, "what becomes of all the things one forgets? Do they — do they go to sleep in one's head?"

Mrs. Harmon looked at him in surprise, for it was by far the most thoughtful question he had ever asked. She could not answer it at once, and he went on.

"Because you always tell me to try and remember, and you think I could remember if I tried hard enough. Then you must believe the things are there. You wouldn't expect me to give you what I hadn't got, would you? That wouldn't be fair."

"No, certainly not," answered his mother, considerably puzzled.

"Then you really think that I don't forget. You must think I don't remember to remember. Something like that. I can't explain what I mean, but you understand."

"I suppose so, my dear. Something like that. Yes, perhaps it is just as you say, and things go to sleep in one's head and one has to wake them up. But I know that I can often remember things I have forgotten if I try very hard."

"I can't. I say, mother, I suppose I'm stupid, though you never tell me so. I know I'm different from other people, somehow. I wish you would tell me just what it is. I don't want to be different from other people. Of course I know I could never be as clever as you, nor the colonel. But then you're awfully clever, both of you. Father used to call me an idiot, but I'm not. I saw an idiot once, and his eyes turned in, and he couldn't shut his mouth, and he couldn't talk properly."

"Are you sure that your father ever called you an idiot, Archie?"

Helen's lips were oddly pale, and her voice was low. Archie laughed in a wooden way.

"Oh, yes! I'm quite sure," he said. "I remember, because he hit me on the back of the head with the knob of his stick when he said so. That was the first time. Then he got into the way of saying it. I wasn't very big then."

Helen leaned back and closed her eyes, and in her mind she saw the word 'forgiven' as she had written it after his name, — 'Henry Harmon, New York. Forgiven.' It had a strange look. She had not known that he had ever struck the boy cruelly.

"Why did you never tell me?" she asked slowly.

"Oh, I don't know. It would have been like a cry-a-baby to go running to you. I just waited."

Helen did not guess what was coming.

"Did he strike you again with the knob of his stick?" she asked.

"Lots of times, with all sorts of things. Once, when you were off somewhere for two or three days on a visit, he came at me with a poker. That was the last time. I suppose he had been drinking more than usual."

"What happened?" asked Helen.

"Oh, well, I'd grown big then, and I got sick of it all at once, you know. He never tried to touch me again, after that."

Helen recalled distinctly that very unusual occasion when she had been absent for a whole week, at the time of a sister's death. Harmon had seemed ill when she had returned, and she remembered noticing a great change in his manner towards the boy only a few months before he had become insane.

"What did you do?" she asked.

"I hit him. I hit him badly, a good many times. Then I put him to bed. I knew he wouldn't tell."

Archie smiled slowly at the recollection of beating his father, and looked down at his fist. Helen felt as though she were going mad herself. It was all horribly unnatural,—the father's cruel brutality to his afflicted son, the son's ferocious vengeance upon his father when he had got his strength.

"You see," continued Archie, "I knew exactly how many times he had hit me altogether, and I gave all the hits back at once. That was fair, anyhow."

Helen could not remember that he had ever professed to be sure of an exact number from memory.

"How could you know just how many

times—" She spoke faintly, and stopped, half sick.

"Blocks," answered Archie. "I dropped a little blot of ink on one of my blocks every time he hit me. I used to count the ones that had blots on them every morning. When they all had one blot each, I began on the other side, till I got round again. Some had blots on several sides at last. I don't know how many there were, now; but it was all right, for I used to count them every morning and remember all day. There must have been forty or fifty, I suppose. But I know it was all right. I didn't want to be unfair, and I hit him slowly and counted. Oh,"—his eyes brightened suddenly, —"I've got the blocks here. I'll go and get them, and we can count them together. Then you'll know exactly."

Helen could not say anything, and Archie was gone. She only half understood what the blocks were, and did not care to know. There was an unnatural horror in it all, and Archie spoke of it quite simply and without any particular resentment. She was still half dazed when he came back with the mysterious box in which he kept his toys.

He set it down on the floor at her feet and knelt beside it, feeling for the key in his pocket.

"I don't care if you see all the things now," he said. "They don't amuse me any more."

Nevertheless, she saw the blush of shame rising to his forehead as he bent down and put the key into the lock.

"I don't care, after all," he said, before he lifted the lid. "It's only you, mother, and you won't think I was a baby just because they amused me. I don't care for them any more, mother. Indeed I don't; so I may as well make a clean breast of it and tell you. Besides, you must see the blocks. All the blots are there still, quite plain, and we can count them, and then you'll always remember, though I shan't. Here they are. I've carried them about a long time, you know, and they're getting pretty old, especially the soldiers. There isn't much paint left on them, and the captain's head's gone."

Helen leaned forward, her elbow on her knees, her chin resting on her hand, her eyes dim, and her heart beating oddly. It seemed as though nothing were spared her on that day.

Archie unpacked the toys in silence, and arranged the blocks all on one side in a neat pile, while on the other he laid the soldiers and the little cart, with the few remaining toys. Helen's eyes became riveted on the bits of wood. There were about twenty of them, and she could plainly distinguish on them the little round blots which

Archie had made, one for each blow he had received. He began to count, and Helen followed him mechanically. He was very methodical, for he knew that he was easily confused. When he had counted the blots on each block, he put it behind him on the floor before he took another from the pile. He finished at last.

"Sixty-three — ju — !" He checked himself. "I forgot. I won't say 'jukes' any more. I won't. There were sixty-three in all, mother. Besides, I remember now. Yes; there were sixty-three. I remember that it took a long time, because I was afraid of not being fair."

Again he smiled at the recollection, with some satisfaction, perhaps, at his conscientious rectitude. With those hands of his, it was a wonder that he had not killed his father. Helen sat like a stone figure, and watched him unconsciously, while her thoughts ground upon each other in her heart like millstones, and her breath half choked her.

He swept all the blocks back in front of him, and, by force of habit, he began to build a little house before he put them away. She watched his strong hands, that could do such childish things, and the bend of his athletic neck. His head was not ill-shaped nor defective under the thick short hair.

"Did he always strike you on the head, Archie?" she asked suddenly.

He knocked the little house over with a sweep of his hand and looked up.

"Generally," he said quietly. "But it doesn't matter, you know. He generally went for the back of my head because it didn't make any mark, as I have such thick hair, so I hit him in the same place. It's all right. It was quite fair. I say, mother, I'm going to throw these things away, now that you know all about them. What's the good of keeping them, anyway? I'm sure I don't know why I ever liked them."

"Give them to me," answered Helen. "Perhaps some poor child might like them."

But she knew that she meant to keep them.

"Well, there isn't much paint on those tin soldiers, you know. I don't believe any child would care for them much. At least not so much as I did, because I was used to them. Of course that made a difference. But you may have them, if you like. I don't want them any more. They're only in the way."

"Give them to me, for the present."

"All right, mother." And he began to pack the toys into the box.

He did it very carefully and neatly, for the habit was strong, though the memory was weak.

Still Helen watched him, without changing her attitude. He sighed as he put in the last of the tin soldiers.

"I suppose I shall really never care for them again," he said.

He looked at them with a sort of affection and touched some of the things lightly, arranging them a little better. Then he shut the lid down, turned the key, and held it out to his mother.

"There you are," he said. "Anyhow, the blocks helped me to remember. Sixty-three, wasn't it, mother?"

"Sixty-three," repeated Helen, mechanically.

Then, for the second time on that evening, she turned her face to the cushion of her chair, and shook from head to foot, and sobbed aloud. She had realized what the number meant. Sixty-three times, in the course of years, had Henry Harmon struck his son upon the head. It was strange that Archie should have any wits at all, and it was no wonder that they were not like those of other men. And it had all been a secret, kept by the child first, then by the growing boy, then by the full-grown man, till his thews and sinews had toughened upon him and he had turned and paid back blow for blow, all at once. And last of all the father had struck her, with a thought of revenge, perhaps, as well as in passion, because he dared not raise his hand against his strong son.

Again she saw the words of her telegram, 'Henry Harmon, New York. Forgiven,' and they were in letters of fire that her tears could not quench. She had not known how much she was forgiving. Archie knelt beside her in wonder, for he had never seen her cry in his life. He touched her arm lovingly, trying to see her face, and his own softened strangely, growing more human as it grew more childlike.

"Don't, mother! Please don't cry like that! If I had thought you would cry about it, I'd never have told you. Besides, it couldn't have hurt him so very much —"

"Him!"

Helen's voice rang out, and she turned, with a fierce light in her angry eyes. In a quick movement her arms ran round Archie's neck and drew him passionately to her breast, and she kissed his head, again and again, always his head, upon the short, thick hair, till he wondered, and laughed.

When they were quiet again, sitting side by side, her battle began once more, and she knew that it must all be fought over on different ground. She had forgiven Henry Harmon, as well as she could, for her own wrongs; but there were others now, and they seemed worse to her than anything she had suffered. It was just to think so, too, for she knew that at any time she could have left Harmon without blame or stain. It had been in her power, but she had chosen not to do it.

But the boy had been powerless and silent through long years. She had never even guessed that his father had ever struck him cruelly. At the merest suspicion of such a thing she would have turned upon her husband as only mothers do turn, tigresses or women. But Archie had kept his secret, while his strength quietly grew upon him, and then he had paid the long score with his own hands. Out of shame, Harmon had kept the secret, too.

Yet she had said in one word that she forgave him, and the word determined the rest of her life. A suffering, a short, sad respite, and then suffering again; that was to sum the history of her years. She must suffer to the end, more and more.

And all at once it seemed to her that she could not bear it. For herself she might have forgiven anything. She had pardoned all for herself, from the first neglect to the scar on her forehead. But it was another matter to forgive for Archie. Why should she? What justice could there be in that? What right had she to absolve Harmon for his cruelty to her child?

She must ask Archie if he forgave his father. She could no longer decide the question alone, and Archie had the best of rights to be consulted. Wimpole's words came back to her, asking whether it could do Archie any good to be under the same roof with his father; and all at once she saw that her whole married life had been centred in her son much more than in herself.

Besides, he must be told that his father had recovered, for every one must know it soon, and people would speak of it before him, and think it very strange if he were ignorant of it. She hid from herself the underthought that Archie must surely refuse to live with his father, after all that had passed, and the wild hope of escape from what she had undertaken to do, which the suggestion raised.

She sat silent and thoughtful, her tears drying on her cheeks, while her son still knelt beside her. But without looking at him, she laid her hand on his arm, and her grasp tightened while she was thinking.

"What is it, mother? What is it?" he asked again and again.

At last she let her eyes go to his, and she answered him.

"Your father is well again. By this time he must have left the asylum. Shall we go back to him?"

"I suppose we must, if he's all right," answered Archie, promptly.

Helen's face fell suddenly, for she had expected a strong refusal.

"Can you forgive him for all he did to you?" she asked slowly.

"I don't see that there's much to forgive. He hit me, and I hit him just as often; so we're square. He won't hit me now, because he's afraid of me. I hate him, of course, and he hates me. It's quite fair. He thinks I'm stupid, and I think he's mean; but I don't see that there's anything to forgive him. I suppose he's made so. If he's all right again, I don't see but what we shall have to go and live with him again. I don't see what you're going to do about it, mother."

Helen buried her face in her hands, not sobbing again, but thinking. She did not see 'what she was going to do about it,' as Archie expressed the situation. If she had not already sent the telegram, it would have been different. The young man's rough phrases showed that he had not the slightest fear of his father, and he was ignorant of what she herself had suffered. Much she had hidden from him altogether, and his dulness had seen nothing of the rest. He supposed, if he thought anything about it, that his mother had been unhappy because Harmon drank hard, and stayed away from home unaccountably, and often spoke roughly and rudely when he had been drinking. To his unsensitive nature and half-developed mind these things had seemed regrettable, but not so very terrible, after all. Helen had been too loyal to hold up Harmon as an example of evil to his son, and the boy had grown up accustomed to what disgusted and revolted her, as well as ignorant of what hurt her; while his own unfinished character was satisfied with a half-barbarous conception of what was fair so far as he himself was concerned. He had given blow for blow and bruise for bruise, and on a similar understanding he was prepared to return to similar conditions. Helen saw it all in a flash, but she could not forgive Harmon.

"I can't! I can't!" she repeated aloud, and she pressed Archie's arm again.

"Can't — what, mother?" he asked. "Can't go back?"

"How can I, after this? How can I ever bear to see him, to touch his hand, — his hand that hurt you, Archie, — that hurt you so much more than you ever dream of?"

There were tears in her voice again, and again

she pressed him close to her. But he did not understand.

"Oh, that's all right, mother," he answered. "Don't cry about me! I made it all right with him long ago. And I don't suppose he hurt me more than I dreamed of, either. That's only a way of talking, you know. It used to make me feel rather stupid. But then, I'm stupid anyway; so even that didn't matter much." And Archie smiled indifferently.

"More than you think, more than you know!" She kissed his hair. "It was that — it may have been that — it must have been — I know it was —"

She was on the point of breaking down again.

"What?" he asked with curiosity. "What do you mean? I don't understand."

Helen's voice sank low, and she hardly seemed to be speaking to her son.

"Your father made you what you are," she said, and her face grew cold and hard.

"What? Stupid?" asked Archie, cheerfully. Then his face changed, too. "I say, mother," he went on, in another voice, "do you think I'm so dull because he hit me on the head?"

Helen repented her words, scarcely knowing why, but sure that it would have been better not to speak them. She did not answer the question.

"That's what you think," said Archie. "And it's because I'm not like other people that you say it's absurd of me to want to marry Sylvia Strahan, isn't it? And that's my father's doing? Is that what you think?"

He waited for an answer, but none came at once. Helen was startled by the clear sequence of ideas, far more logical than most of his reasonings. It seemed as if his sudden passion for Sylvia had roused his sluggish intelligence from its long torpor. She could not deny the truth of what he said, and he saw that she could not.

"That's it," he continued. "That's what you think. I knew it."

His brows knitted themselves straight across his forehead, and his eyes were fixed upon his mother's face, as he knelt beside her. She had not been looking at him, but she turned to him slowly now.

"And that's why you ask whether I can forgive him," he concluded.

"Can you?"

"No."

He rose to his feet from his knees easily, by one movement, and she watched him. Then there was a long silence and he began to walk up and down.

Helen felt as if she had done something disloyal, and that he had given the answer for which she had been longing intensely, as an escape from her decision, and as a means of freedom from bondage to come. She could ask herself now what right she had to expect that Archie should forgive his father. But, instead, she asked what right she could have had to give Archie so good a reason for hating him, when the boy had not suspected that which, after all, might not be the truth. She had made an enormous sacrifice in sending the message of forgiveness for her own wrongs, but it seemed to her, all at once, that in rousing Archie's resentment for his own injuries she had marred the purity of her own intention.

Indeed she was in no state to judge herself, for what Archie had told her was a goad in her wound, with a terror of new pain.

"You cannot forgive him," she said mechanically and almost to herself.

"Why should I?" asked Archie. "It means Sylvia to me. How can I forgive him that?"

And suddenly, without waiting for any answer, he went out and left her alone.

After a long time, she wrote this letter to her husband:

DEAR HENRY,—I am very glad to hear of your recovery, and I have received your letter to-day, together with the doctor's. I have telegraphed the one word for which you asked, and you have probably got the message already. But I must answer your letter as well as I can, and say a great many things which I shall never say again. If we are to meet and try to live together, it is better that I should speak plainly before I see you.

You asked a great deal of me, and for myself I have done what you asked. I do not say this to make it seem as though I were making a great sacrifice and wished you to admit it. We were not happy together; you say that it was your fault, and you ask me to forgive you. If I believed that you had been in full possession of your senses till you were taken ill, I do not think that forgiveness could be possible. You see, I am frank. I am sure that you often did not know what you said and did, and that when you did know, you could not always weigh the consequences of your words and actions. So I will try to forget them. That is what you mean by being forgiven, and it is the only meaning either you or I can put upon the word. I will try to forget, and I will bear no malice for anything in the past, so far as I am concerned. Never speak of it, when we meet, and I never will. If you really wish to try the experiment of living together again, I am willing to attempt it, as an experiment.

But there is Archie to be considered, and Archie will not forgive you. By a mere chance, to-day, after I had sent my telegram, he told me that you used to strike him cruelly and often because his dulness irritated you. You struck him on the head, and you injured his brain, so that his mind has never developed fully and never can.

I do not think that if I were a man, as he is, I could forgive that. Could you? Do you expect that I should, being his mother? You cannot. You and he can never live under the same roof again. It would perhaps be harder for you, feeling as you must, than for him; but in any case it is not possible, and there is only one arrangement to be made. We must put Archie in some place where he shall be safe and healthy and happy, and I will spend a part of the year with you and a part with him. I will not give him up for you, and I am not willing to give you up for him. Neither would be right. You are my husband, whatever there may have been in the past; but Archie is my child. It will be harder for me than for him, too.

You say that I might have got a divorce from you, and you do me the justice to add that you believe I have never thought of it. That is true, but it is not a proof of affection. I have none for you. I told you that I should speak plainly, and it is much better. It would be an ignoble piece of comedy on my part to pretend to be fond of you. I was once. I admired you, I suppose, and I liked you well enough to marry you, being rather ignorant of the world and of what people could feel. If you had really loved me and been kind to me, I should have loved you in the end. But, as it turned out, I could not go on admiring you long, and I simply ceased to like you. That is our story, and it is a sad one. We made the great mistake, for we married without much love on either side, and we were very young.

But it was a marriage, just the same, and a bond which I never meant to break and will not break now. A promise is a promise, whatever happens, and a vow made before God is ten times a promise. So I always mean to keep mine to you, as I have kept it. I will do my best to make you happy, and you must do your part to make it possible.

After all, that is the way most people live. True love, lasting lifetimes and not changing, exists in the world, and it is the hope of it that makes youth lovely and marriage noble. Few people find it, and the many who do not must live as well as they can without it. That is what we must do. Perhaps, though the hope of love is gone, we may find peace together. Let us try.

But not with Archie. There are things which no woman can forgive nor forget. I could not forgive you this if I loved you with all my heart, and you must not expect it of me, for it is not in my power. The harm was not done to me, but to him, and he is more to me than you ever were, and far more to me than myself. I will only say that. There can be no need of ever speaking about it, but I want you to understand; and not only this, but everything. That is why I write such a long letter.

It must all be perfectly clear, and I hope I have made it so. It was I who suffered for the great mistake we made in marrying, but you are sorry for that, and I say, let us try the experiment and see whether we can live together in peace for the rest of our lives. You are changed since your illness, I have no doubt, and you will make it as easy as you can. At least, you will do your best, and so shall I.

Have I repeated myself in this letter? At least, I have tried to be clear and direct. Besides, you know me, and you know what I mean by writing in this way. I am in earnest.

God bless you, Henry. I hope this may turn out well. HELEN.

It was ten o'clock when she had finished. She laid her hand upon the bell, meaning to send her letter to the post office by a servant; but just then the sound of laughing voices came up to her through the open window, and she did not ring. Looking out, she saw that there were still many people in the street, for it was a warm evening. It was only a step from her hotel to the post office, and if she went herself she should have the satisfaction of knowing positively that the letter was safe. She put on a hat with a thick veil, and went out.

CHAPTER IX

COLONEL WIMPOLE looked positively old that evening when he went down to dinner with his sister and Sylvia. His face was drawn and weary and the lids hung a little, in small wrinkles; but down in his grey eyes there was a far-off gleam of danger-light.

Sylvia looked down when she met him, and she was very silent and grave at first. At dinner she sat between him and Miss Wimpole, and for some time she scarcely dared to glance at him. He, on his part, was too much preoccupied to speak much, and she thought he was displeased. Nevertheless, he was more than usually thoughtful for her. She understood by the way he sat, and even by the half-unconscious shrinking of the elbow next to her, that he was sorry for her. At table, seated close together, there is a whole language in one's neighbour's elbow and an unlimited power of expression in its way of avoiding collisions. Very perceptive people understand that. Primarily, in savage life, the bold man turns his elbows out, while the timid one presses them to his sides, as though not to give offence with them. Society teaches us to put on some little airs of timidity as a substitute for the modesty that few feel, and we accordingly draw in our elbows when we are near any one. It is ridiculous enough, but there are a hundred ways of doing it, a hundred degrees of readiness, unwillingness, pride, or consideration for others, as well as sympathy for their troubles or in their successes, all of which are perfectly natural to refined people, and almost entirely unconscious. The movement of a man's jaws at dinner shows much of his real character, but the movement of his elbows shows with fair accuracy the degree of refinement in which he has been brought up.

Sylvia was sure that the colonel was sorry for her, and the certainty irritated her, for she hated to be pitied, and most of all for having done something foolish. She glanced at Wimpole's tired face, just when he was looking a little away from her, and she was startled by the change in his features since the early afternoon. It needed no very keen perception to see that he was in profound anxiety of some kind, and she knew of nothing which could have disturbed him deeply but her own conduct.

Under the vivid light of the public dining table, he looked old. That was undeniable, and it was really the first time that Sylvia had definitely connected the idea of age with him. Just beyond him sat a man in the early prime of strength, one of those magnificent specimens of humanity such as one sees occasionally in travelling but whom one very rarely knows in acquaintance. He could not have been more than twenty-eight years old, straight in his seat, broad-shouldered, with thick, close, golden hair and splendid golden beard, white forehead and sunburned cheeks, broad, well-modelled brows and faultless nose, and altogether manly in spite of his beauty. As he leaned forward a little, his fresh young face appeared beside the colonel's tired profile, in vivid contrast.

For the first time, Sylvia realized the meaning of Wimpole's words, spoken that afternoon. He might almost have been her grandfather, and he was in reality of precisely the same age as her father. Sylvia looked down again and reflected that she must have made a mistake with herself. Youth can sometimes close its eyes to grey hair, but it can never associate the idea of love with old age, when clearly brought to its perceptions.

For at least five minutes the world seemed utterly hollow to Sylvia, as she sat there. She did not even wonder why she had thought the colonel young until then. The sudden dropping out of her first great illusion left a void as big and as hollow as itself.

She turned her head, and looked once more, and there, again, was the glorious, unseamed youth of the stranger, almost dazzling her and making the poor colonel look more than ever old, with his pale, furrowed cheeks and wrinkled eyelids. She thought a moment, and then she was sure that she could never like such a terribly handsome young man; and at the same instant, for the first time in her life, she felt that natural, foolish, human pity which only extreme youth feels for old age, and she wondered why she had not always felt it, for it seemed quite natural, and was altogether in accordance with the rest of her feelings for the colonel, with her reverence for his perfect character, her admiration for his past deeds, her attachment to his quiet, protective, wise, and all-gentle manliness. That was her view of his qualities, and she had to admit that though he had them all, he was what she called old. She had taken for love what was only a combination of reverence and attachment and admiration. She realized her mistake in a flash, and it seemed to her that the core had withered in the fruit of the universe.

Just then the colonel turned to her, holding his glass in his hand.

"We must not forget that it is your birthday, my dear," he said, and his natural smile came back. "Rachel," he added, speaking to his sister across the young girl, "let us drink Sylvia's health on her eighteenth birthday."

Miss Wimpole usually took a little thin Moselle with the cold water she drank. She solemnly raised the glass, and inclined her head as she looked first at Sylvia and then at the colonel.

"Thank you," said Sylvia, rather meekly.

Then they all relapsed into silence. The people at the big table talked fast, in low tones, and the clattering of dishes and plates and knives and forks went on steadily and untunefully all around. Sylvia felt lonely in the unindividual atmosphere of the Swiss hotel. She hated the terribly handsome young man, with a mortal hatred, because he made the colonel look old. She could not help seeing him whenever she turned towards Wimpole. At last she spoke softly, looking down at her plate.

"Uncle Richard," she said, to call his attention.

He was not really her uncle, and she almost always called him 'colonel,' half playfully, and because she had hated the suggestion of age that is conveyed by the word 'uncle.' Wimpole turned to her quietly.

"Yes, my dear," he said. "What is it?"

"I suppose I was very foolish to-day, wasn't I?" asked Sylvia, very low indeed, and a bright blush played upon her pretty face.

The colonel was a courteous man, and was also very fond of her.

"A woman need never be wise when she is lovely," he said in his rather old-fashioned way, and he smiled affectionately at the young girl. "It is quite enough if she is good."

But she did not smile. On the contrary, her face became very grave.

"I am in earnest," she said, and she waited a moment before saying more. "I was very foolish," she continued, thoughtfully. "I did not understand — or I did not realize — I don't know. You have been so much to me all my life, and there is nobody like you, of course. It seemed to me — I mean, it seems to me — that is very much like really caring for some one, isn't it? You know what I mean. I can't express it."

"You mean that it is a good deal like love, I suppose," answered the colonel, speaking gravely now. "Yes, I suppose that love is better when people believe each other to be angels. But it is not that sort of thing which makes love what it is."

"What is it, then?" Sylvia was glad to

ask any question that helped to break through the awkwardness and embarrassment she felt towards him.

"There are a great many kinds of love," he said; "but I think there is only one kind worth having. It is the kind that begins when one is young, and lasts all one's life."

"Is that all?" asked Sylvia, innocently, and in a disappointed tone.

"All!" The colonel laughed softly, and a momentary light of happiness came into his face, for that all was all he had ever had. "Is not that enough, my dear?" he asked. "To love one woman or man with all one's heart for thirty or forty years? Never to be disappointed? Never to feel that one has made a mistake? Never to fear that love may grow old because one grows old oneself? Is not that enough?"

"Ah, yes! That would be, indeed. But you did not say all those other things at first."

"They are just what make a life-long love," answered the colonel. "But then," he added, "there are a great many degrees, far below that. I am sure I have seen people quite really in love with each other for a week."

Sylvia suddenly looked almost angry as she glanced at him.

"That sort of thing ought not to be called love at all!" she answered energetically. "It is nothing but a miserable flirtation, — a miserable, wretched, unworthy flirtation."

"I quite agree with you," said Wimpole, smiling at her vehemence.

"Why do you laugh?" she asked, almost offended by his look. His smile disappeared instantly.

"You hit the world very hard, my dear," he answered.

"I hate the world!" cried Sylvia.

She was just eighteen. Wimpole knew that she felt an innocent and instinctive repulsion for what the world meant to him, and for all the great, sinful unknown. He disliked it himself, with the steady, subdued dislike which is hatred in such natures as his, both because it was contrary to his character, and for Sylvia's sake, who must surely one day know something of it. So he did not laugh at her sweeping declaration. She hated the world before knowing it, but he hated it in full knowledge. That was a bond of sympathy like any other. To each of us the world means both what we know, and what we suspect, both what we see and the completion of it in the unseen, both the outward lives of our companions which we can judge, and their inward motives, which we dimly guess.

But on this evening Sylvia felt that the world was particularly odious, for she had suffered a first humiliation in her own eyes. She thought that she had lowered herself in the colonel's estimation, and she had discovered that she had made a great mistake with herself about him.

"I hate the world!" she repeated, in a lower tone, almost to herself, and her eyes gleamed with young anger, while her delicate, curving lips just showed her small white teeth.

Wimpole watched her face.

"That is no reason for hating yourself," he said gently.

She started and turned her eyes to him. Then she blushed and looked away.

"You must not guess my thoughts," she answered. "It is not kind."

"I did not mean to. I am sorry."

"Oh — you could not help it, of course. I was so foolish to-day."

The blush deepened, and she said nothing more. The colonel returned to his own secret trouble, and on Sylvia's other side Miss Wimpole was silently planning a charitable institution of unusual severity, while she peeled an orange with the most scrupulous neatness and precision.

CHAPTER X

SYLVIA went to her own room after dinner, still wondering what had happened to her on her birthday. There is an age at which most of us unexpectedly come across the truth about ourselves, and sometimes about others, and it generally happens that in our recollection the change turns upon one day, or even one hour.

The shock is sudden and unexpected. Floating down a quick smooth stream in a boat, a man is aware of motion, as he watches the bank without realizing the strength of the flowing water; but when the skiff is suddenly checked by any obstacle in midstream, the whole force of the river rushes upon it, and past it, and perhaps over it, in an instant. Something of the same sort happens now and then in our lives. The great illusion of childhood carries us along at a speed of which we have no idea, in the little boat which is the immediate and undeniable reality of near surroundings, the child's cradle afloat upon a fiction which is wide and deep and strong, and sometimes we are grown men and women before our small craft strikes upon a shoal of truth, with a dash that throws us from the thwart, and frightens the bravest of us. There we stick fast upon the rough fact for a while, and the flood that was so smooth and pleasant rushes past us, foaming and seething and breaking against the boat's side and threatening to tear her to pieces. And if the tide is ebbing at the river's mouth, we may be left high and dry upon the sharp reality for a long time; but if not, the high water will presently float us, and off we shall spin again, smoothly and safely, on the bosom of the sweet untrue.

Such accidents happen more than once to most people, and almost every one resents them bitterly. Even in daily living, few men can bear to be roughly roused from sleep. Much more is the waking rude from year-long dreams of fancy.

Sylvia sat at her table and stared at the lamp, as if it were her own heart which she could look into, and watch, and study, and criticise. For most of all, she was in a humour to find fault with it, as having played her false when she least expected that it could deceive her. She had built on it, as it dictated; she had trusted it, as it suggested; she had lived, and loved to live, for its sake; and now it had betrayed her. It had not been in earnest, all the time, but had somehow made her think that she herself was all earnestness. It was a false and silly little heart, and she hated it, as she looked at it in the lamp, and she wished that it would frizzle and burn like the poor moth that had gone too near the hot glass while she had been downstairs.

It was positively laughing at her, now, and she set her small mouth angrily. To think that she should ever have fancied herself in love with a man who might have been her grandfather! And it wickedly showed her the colonel as he would be in another ten years, a picture founded upon the tired look she had just seen in his face. She was ashamed of herself, and furious against herself for being ashamed, and she suddenly wished that she were dead, because that would give people a real reason for being sorry for her. It would be very pathetic to die so young! If she did, her heart could not laugh at her.

She thought about it for a while, and among other reflexions she suddenly found herself wondering whether young Knox, the officer on her father's ship, would be very sorry. He had written her a letter from Japan which she had not answered. Indeed, she was not sure that she had read every word of it, for it had only come this morning. Life had been too short for reading letters on that day. But there it was, on the table. She had the evening before her, and though it was a long letter, it could not take more than a quarter of an hour to go through it. She put out her hand to take it and then looked at the lamp again.

A lean, brown young face was suddenly there, and bright eyes that looked straight at her, without anything vastly superior in them, but full of something she liked and understood and instantly longed for. Her heart was not laughing at her any more, for she had forgotten all about it, which is generally the best thing one can do in such cases.

Even the expression of her face changed and softened as she laid her hand upon the letter. For Wimpole's sake, as she had made herself think a few hours earlier, she would gladly have doubled her age, and the forced longing for equality of years between herself and her ideal had fleetingly expressed itself in her face by shadows, where there could not yet be lines. But as the illusion sank down into the storehouse of all impossibilities and all mistakes, the light of early youth fell full and unscreened upon her face again, and she revived unconsciously, as day-flowers do at sunrise, when the night-flowers fold their leaves.

It was surely no thought of love which made the change; or if that were its cause, it was but love's fore-lightening in a waking dream. Much rather it must have been the consciousness of living roused by the thought of youth. For youth is the elixir of life, and the touch of old age is a blight on youth, when youth is longing to be old; but youth that is willingly young has power to give the old a breath of itself again, before the very end. In their children men live again, and in their children's children they remember the loveliness of childhood.

From a very far country, across half a world of land and water, the letter had come to Sylvia on her birthday, as Harmon's had come to Helen. There is something strange and terrible, if we realize it, in man's power to harm or help by written words from any distance. The little bit of paper leaves our hand with its wishing-carpet in the shape of a postage stamp, and swiftly singles out the one man or woman, in two thousand millions, for whom it is meant, going straight to its mark with an aim far more unerring than steel or ball. A man may much more probably miss his enemy with a pistol at ten paces, than with a letter at ten thousand miles. If the fabled inhabitant of Mars could examine our world under an imaginary glass, as we study a drop of water under a microscope, he would surely be profoundly interested in the movements of the letter-bacillus, as he might call it. He might question whether it is generated spontaneously, or is the result of an act of will, more or less aggressive, but he would marvel at the rapidity of its motion and at the strength of its action upon the human animal through the eye. It would be very inexplicable to him; least of all could he understand the instant impulse of man to tear off the shell of the bacillus as soon as it reaches him, for he would no doubt notice that in a vast number of cases the sight of it produces discontent and pain, and he might even find a few instances in which death followed almost immediately. In others the bacteria produce amazingly exhilarating results, such as laughter and the undignified antics of joy, and even sudden improvements in the animal's health and appearance. He would especially notice that these bacilli are almost perpetually in motion, from the time they leave one human being until they fasten themselves upon another, and that in parts of the world where they are not found at all, or only sporadically, the animals behave in a very different way, are healthier, and are less exposed to the fatal results of their own inventions. If the inhabitant of Mars were given to jumping at conclusions, he would certainly announce to his fellow-beings that he had discovered in Earth the germ of a disease called by Terrenes 'Civilization.' And perhaps that is just what the letter is.

Young Knox wrote to Sylvia because he was in love with her, which is the best of all reasons for writing when love is right, and the worst imaginable when it is wrong. He was so much in love that as soon as she was out of his sight his first impulse was to set down on paper all sorts of things which had very little sense in them, but made up for a famine of wisdom by a corresponding plenty of feeling. There is something almost pathetic in the humbleness of a young man's strength before the object of his first true love. It is the abasement of the real before the ideal; but if the ideal fails, the real takes vengeance of the man for having trodden it under.

Young women rarely understand their power; older ones too often overrate what they have. The girl who first breathes the air of the outer world and first sees in a man's eyes that he loves her, knows that he is stronger, better taught, more experienced than she is, and compares herself with him by a measure which he rates as nothing. Man is much more real to woman, when both are very young, than woman is to man; and being real he represents to her a sort of material force. But to him she is an imaginary being, strong with a mystic influence from which he cannot escape when he has come within the pentagram of the spell. It is bad for a man if she comes to know her strength before he has learned his weakness. Then she riots in it, recklessly, for a time, until she has hurt him. She says, 'Do this,' and he does it, like the Centurion's servant; or 'Say this,' and he says it, be the words wise or foolish, and she reckons his wisdom to herself and his folly to him, frankly, and without the least doubt of her own perfection, for a while, rejoicing senselessly in driving him. But by and by, as in a clock, the mainspring feels the gentle regulation of the swaying balance, and the balance takes its motion from the spring, till both together move in perfect time, while each without the other would be but a useless bit of machinery.

Sylvia did not know all that, and if she had, she would perhaps not have reasoned about it much. She did not understand why young Knox wrote that he would live for her, die for her, and, if necessary, convulse the solar system for her exclusive pleasure and benefit. It seemed a great deal to promise under the circumstances, and her moderate maiden vanity could not make her appear, in her own eyes, as an adequate cause of such serious disturbance in the order of things; yet it was not displeasing to be magnified into a possible source of astronomical miracles, though the idea was slightly ridiculous and she was glad that she had it entirely to herself and beyond carping criticism.

She was not in the least in love with the man who wrote to her, and she had not been in love with him when they had parted. That very morning, when she had received the letter, she had been a little inclined to smile at the writer's persistence, and had laid the letter aside, half read, in no great hurry to finish it. But since then, her life had changed. She had gone aground on the shoal of truth and she was already longing for the waters of illusion to rise and float her away.

So she let the breezy memories come back to her, and they brought her a sweet forewarning of her growing life. All at once, she knew that she had never met any one so young who had pleased her so much, any one with such clear eyes and manly ways, frank smile and honest voice, as the young officer who had hated this hollow world with such grave conviction because Sylvia Strahan could not go home in her father's ship. She read on, and felt an unexpected thrill of pleasure when the words told her what she had already known; namely, that the squadron would be far on its way to San Francisco by the time the letter reached her, that Knox was to come to the capital with her father, and that she was quite certain to meet him there before very long. She was unconscious of looking round at her things just then and wishing that they were already packed for the homeward journey.

She wrote to him before she went to bed. It was a duty of civility to answer him, though she felt herself under no obligation to reply to his numerous questions. On the contrary, she said nothing at all about them, but she gave him her impressions of Lucerne and told him that Aunt Rachel had taken cold, but was now quite well, a piece of information which, though satisfactory in its way, was not calculated to affect her correspondent's happiness in any marked degree. 'It would be nice to see each other again,' she said at the end, with which mild sentiment she signed herself 'sincerely' his.

The only odd thing about it all was that when the letter was finished she had not the slightest idea where to send it, a fact which had not crossed her mind when she had unscrewed her travelling inkstand, but which sufficiently proved that she had acted under an impulse of some sort. She said to herself that it did not matter, but she was disappointed, and the smile faded from her face for a little while.

When she was asleep it came back in the

dark and lingered on her lips all night, waning and waxing with her maiden dreams.

Her eighteenth birthday had been a good day in her life, after all. There are few indeed who fall asleep happily when the first illusion has gone down into darkness with the evening sun.

CHAPTER XI

HELEN HARMON went out alone to mail her letter. She would not have done such a thing in any great city of Europe, but there is a sense of safety in the dull, impersonal atmosphere of Lucerne, and it was a relief to her to be out in the open air alone; it would be a still greater relief to have dropped the letter into the mysterious slit which is the first stage on the road to everywhere.

No one ever thinks of the straight little cut, with its metal cover, as being at all tragical. And yet it is as tragic as the jaws of death, in its way. Many a man and woman has stood before it with a letter and hesitated; and every one has, at some time or other, felt the sharp twist at the heart, which is the wrench of the irrevocable, when the envelope has just slipped away into darkness. The words cannot be unwritten any more, after that, nor burned, nor taken back. A telegram may contradict them, or explain them, or ask pardon for them, but the message will inevitably be read, and do its work of peace or war, of challenge or forgiveness, of cruelty, or kindness, or indifference.

Helen did not mean to hesitate, for she hastened towards the moment of looking back upon a deed now hard to do. It was not far to the post office, either, and the thing could soon be done. Yet in her brain there was a surging of uncertainties and a whirling of purposes, in the midst of which she clung hard to her determination, though it should cost ever so dear to carry it out. She had not half thought of all the consequences yet, nor of all it must mean to her to be separated from her son. The results of her action sprang up now, like sudden dangers, and tried to frighten her from her purpose, tried to gain time against her to show themselves, tried to terrify her back to inaction and doubt. Something asked her roughly whence she had got the conviction that she was doing right at all. Another something, more subtle, whispered that she was sacrificing Archie for the sake of her own morbid conscience, and making herself a martyr's crown, not of her own sufferings only, but of her son's loss in losing her. It told her that the letter she held in her hand was a mistake, but not irrevocable until it should have slipped into the dark entrance of the road to everywhere.

She had still a dozen steps to make before

reaching the big white building that stands across the corner of the street, and she was hurrying on, lest she should not reach the door in time. Then she almost ran against Colonel Wimpole, walking slowly along the pavement where there was a half shadow. Both stopped short, and looked at each other in surprise. He saw the letter in her hand, and guessed that she had written to her husband.

"I was only going to the post office," she said, half apologetically, for she thought that he must wonder why she had come out alone at such an hour.

"Will you let me walk with you?" he asked.

"Yes."

He made a step forwards, as though expecting her to turn back from her errand and go with him.

"Not that way," she said. "I must go to the post office first."

"No. Please don't." He placed himself in her way.

"I must."

She spoke emphatically and stood still, facing him, while their eyes met again, and neither spoke again for a few seconds.

"You are ruining your life," he said, after the pause. "When that letter is gone, you will never be able to get it back."

"I know. I shall not wish to."

"You will." His lips set themselves rather firmly as he opposed her, but her face darkened.

"Is this a trial of strength between us?" she asked.

"Yes. I mean to keep you from going back to Henry Harmon."

"I have made up my mind," Helen answered.

"So have I," said Wimpole.

"How can you hinder me? You cannot prevent me from sending this letter, nor from going to him if I choose. And I have chosen to go. That ends it."

"You are mistaken. You are reckoning without me, and I will make it impossible."

"You? How? Even if I send this letter?"

"Yes. Come and walk a little, and we can talk. If you insist upon it, drop your letter into the box. But it will only complicate matters, for you shall not go back to Harmon."

Again she looked at him. He had never spoken in this way, during all the years of their acknowledged friendship and unspoken love. She felt that she resented his words and manner, but at the same time that she loved him better and admired him more. He was stronger and more dominant than she had guessed.

"You have no right to say such things to

me," she answered. "But I will walk with you for a few minutes. Of course you can hinder me from sending my letter now. I can take it to the post office by and by."

"You cannot suppose that I mean to prevent you by force," said Wimpole, and he stood aside to let her pass if she would.

"You said that it was a trial of strength," she answered.

She hesitated one moment, and then turned and began to walk with him. They crossed the street to the side by which the river runs, away from the hotels and the houses. It was darker there and more quiet, and they felt more alone. It would seem easier, too, to talk in the open air, with the sound of the rushing water in their ears. He was the first to speak then.

"I want to explain," he said quietly.

"Yes." She waited for him to go on.

"I suppose that there are times in life when it is better to throw over one's own scruples, if one has any," he began. "I have never done anything to be very proud of, perhaps, but I never did anything to be ashamed of either. Perhaps I shall be ashamed of what I am going to say now. I don't care. I would rather commit a crime than let you wreck your whole existence, but I hope you will not make me do that."

They had stopped in their walk, and were leaning against the railing that runs along the bank.

"You are talking rather desperately," said Helen, in a low voice.

"It is rather a desperate case," Wimpole answered. "I talk as well as I can, and there are things which I must tell you, whatever you think of me; things I never meant to say, but which have made up most of my life. I never meant to tell you."

"What?"

"That I love you. That is the chief thing."

The words did not sound at all like a lover's speech, as he spoke them. He had drawn himself up and stood quite straight, holding the rail with his hands. He spoke coolly, with a sort of military precision, as though he were facing an enemy's fire. There was not exactly an effort in his voice, but the tone showed that he was doing a hard thing at that moment. Then he was silent, and Helen said nothing for a long time. She was leaning over the rail, trying to see the running water in the dark.

"Thank you," she said at last, very simply, and there was another pause.

"I did not expect you to say that," he answered presently.

"Why not? We are not children, you and I. Besides — I knew it."

"Not from me!" Wimpole turned almost sharply upon her.

"No. Not from you. You wrote Henry a letter, many years ago. Do you remember? I had to read everything when he went to the asylum, so I read that, too. He had kept it all those years."

"I am sorry. I never meant you to know. But it does not matter now, since I have told you myself."

He spoke coldly again, almost indifferently, looking straight before him into the night.

"It matters a great deal," said Helen, almost to herself, and he did not hear her.

She kept her head bent down, though he could not have seen her face clearly if she had looked up at him. Her letter burned her, and she hated herself, and loved him. She despised herself, because in the midst of the greatest sacrifice of her life, she had felt the breath of far delight in words that cost him so much. Yet she would have suffered much, even in her good pride, rather than have had them unspoken, for she had unknowingly waited for them half a lifetime. Being a good woman, she was too much a woman to speak one word in return, beyond the simple thanks that sounded so strangely to him, for women exaggerate both good and evil as no man can.

"I know, I know!" he said, suddenly continuing. "You are married, and I should not speak. I believe in those things as much as you do, though I am a man, and most men would laugh at me for being so scrupulous. You ought never to have known, and I meant that you never should. But then, you are married to Harmon still, because you choose to be, and because you will not be free. Does not that make a difference?"

"No, not that. That makes no difference." She raised her head a little.

"But it does now," answered Wimpole. "It is because I do love you, just as I do, with all my heart, that I mean to keep you from him, whether it is right or wrong. Don't you see that right and wrong only matter to one's own miserable self? I shall not care what becomes of my soul if I can keep you from all that unhappiness — from that real danger. It does not matter what becomes of me afterwards — even if I were to go straight to New York and kill Harmon and be hanged for the murder, it would not matter, so long as you were free and safe."

The man had fought in honourable battles, and had killed, and knew what it meant.

"Is that what you intend to do?" asked Helen, and her voice shook.

"It would mean a great deal, if I had to do it," he answered quietly enough. "It would show that I loved you very much. For I have been an honourable man all my life, and have never done anything to be ashamed of. I should be killing a good deal, besides Henry Harmon, but I would give it to make you happy, Helen. I am in earnest."

"You could not make me happy in that way."

"No. I suppose not. I shall find some other way. In the first place, I shall see Harmon and talk to him — "

"How? When?" Helen turned up her face in surprise.

"If you send what you have written, I shall leave to-night," said the colonel. "I shall reach New York as soon as your letter and see Harmon before he reads it, and tell him what I think."

"You will not do that?" She did not know whether she was frightened, or not, by the idea.

"I will," he answered. "I will not stay here tamely and let you wreck your life. If you mail your letter, I shall take the midnight train to Paris. I told you that I was in earnest."

Helen was silent, for she saw a new difficulty and more trouble before her, as though the last few hours had not brought her enough.

"I think," said Wimpole, "that I could persuade Harmon not to accept your generosity."

"I am not doing anything generous. You are making it hard for me to do what is right. You are almost threatening to do something violent, to hinder me."

"No. I know perfectly well that I should never do anything of that sort, and I think you know it, too. To treat Harmon as he deserves would certainly make a scandal which must reflect upon you."

"Please remember that he is still my husband —"

"Yes," interrupted Wimpole, bitterly, "and that is his only title to consideration."

Helen was on the point of rebuking him, but reflected that what he said was probably true.

"Please respect it, then, if you think so," she said quietly. "You say that you care for me — no, I won't put it so — you do care for me. You love me, and I know you do. Let us be perfectly honest with each other. As long as you help me do right, it is not wrong to love me as you do, though I am another man's wife. But as soon as you stand between me and my husband, it is wrong — wicked! It is wicked, no matter what he may have been to me. That has nothing to do with it. It is coming between man and wife —"

"Oh — really — that is going too far!" Wimpole raised his head a little higher, and seemed to breathe the night air angrily through his nostrils.

"No," answered Helen, persistently, for she was arguing against her heart, if not against her head, "it is not going at all too far. Such things should be taken for granted, or at least they should be left to the man and wife in question to decide. No one has any right to interfere, and no one shall. If I can forgive, you can have nothing to resent; for the mere fact of your liking me very much does not give you any sort of right to direct my life, does it? I am glad that you are so fond of me, for I trust you and respect you in every way, and even now I know that you are interfering only because you care for me. But you have not the right to interfere, not the slightest, and although you may be able to, yet if I beg you not to, it will not be honourable of you to come between us."

Colonel Wimpole moved a little impatiently.

"I will take my honour into my own hands," he said.

"But not mine," answered Helen.

They looked at each other in the gloom, as they leaned upon the railing.

"Yours shall be quite safe," said the colonel slowly. "But if you will drop that letter into the river, you will make things easier in every way."

"I should write it over again. Besides, I have telegraphed to him already."

"What? Cabled?"

"Yes. You see that you can do nothing to hinder me. He has my message already. The matter is decided."

She bent her head again, looking down into the rushing water as though tired of arguing.

"You are a saint," said the colonel. "I could not have done that."

"Perhaps I could not, if I had waited," answered Helen, in a voice so low that he could hardly hear the words. "But it is done now," she added, still lower, so that he could not hear at all.

Wimpole had been a man of quick decisions so long as he had been a soldier, but since then he had cultivated the luxury of thinking slowly. He began to go over the situation, trying to see what he could do, not losing courage yet, but understanding how very hard it would be to keep Helen from sacrificing herself.

And she peered down at the black river, that rushed past with a cruel sound, as though it were tearing away the time of freedom, second by second. It was done, now, as she had said. She knew herself too well to believe that even if she should toss the letter into the stream, she would not write another in just such words. But the regret was deep, and thrilled with a secret, aching pulse of its own, all through her, and she thought of what life might have been, if she had not made the great mistake, and of what it still might be if she did not go back to her husband. The man who stood beside her loved her, and was ready to give everything, perhaps even to his honour, to save her from unhappiness. And she loved him, too, next to honour. In the tranquil life she was leading, there could be a great friendship between them, such as few people can even dream of. She knew him, and she knew herself, and she believed it possible, for once in the history of man and woman. In a measure, it might subsist, even after she had gone back to Harmon, but not in the same degree, for between the two men there would be herself. Wimpole would perhaps refuse altogether to enter Harmon's door or to touch Harmon's hand. And then, in her over-scrupulousness, during the time she was to spend with Archie, she knew that she should hesitate to receive freely a man who would not be on speaking terms with the husband whom she had taken back, no matter how she felt towards Wimpole.

Besides, he had told her that he loved her,

and that made a difference, too. So long as the word had never been spoken, there had been the reasonable doubt to shield her conscience. His old love might, after all, have turned to friendship, which is like the soft, warm ashes of wood when the fire is quite burned out. But he had spoken at last, and there was no more doubt, and his quiet words had stirred her own heart. He had begun by telling her that he had many things to say; but, after all, the one and only thing he had said which he had never said before was that he loved her.

It was enough, and too much, and it made everything harder for her. We speak of struggles with ourselves. It would really be far more true to talk of battles between our two selves, or even sometimes between our threefold natures, — our good, our bad, and our indifferent personalities.

To Helen, the woman who loved Richard Wimpole was not the woman who meant to go back to Henry Harmon; and neither, perhaps, was quite the same individual as the mother of poor Archie. The three were at strife with one another, though they were one being in suffering. For it is true that we may be happy in part, and in part be indifferent; but no real pain of the soul leaves room for any happiness at all, or indifference, while it lasts.

So soon as we can be happy again, even for a moment, the reality of the pain is over, though the memory of it may come back now and then in cruel little day-dreams, after years. Happiness is composite; pain is simple. It may take a hundred things to make a man happy, but it never needs more than one to make him suffer. Happiness is, in part, elementary of the body; but pain is only of the soul, and its strength is in its singleness. Bodily suffering is the opposite of bodily pleasure; but true pain has no true opposite, nor reversed counterpart, of one unmixed composition, and the dignity of a great agony is higher than all the glories of joy.

"Promise me that you will not do anything to hinder me," said Helen at last.

"I cannot." There was no hesitation in the answer.

"But if I ask you," she said; "if I beg you, if I entreat you —"

"It is of no use, Helen. I should do my best to keep you away from Harmon, even if I were sure that you would never speak to me nor see me again. I have said almost all I can, and so have you. You are half a saint, or altogether one, or you could not do what you are doing. But I am not. I am only a man. I don't like to talk about myself much, but I would not have you think that I care a straw for my own happiness compared with yours. I would rather know that you were never to see Harmon again than —" He stopped short.

"Than what?" asked Helen, after a pause.

He did not answer at once, but stood upright again beside her, grasping the rail.

"No matter, if you do not understand," he said at last. "Can I give you any proof that it is not for myself, because I love you, that I want to keep you from Harmon? Shall I promise you that when I have succeeded I will not see you again as long as I live?"

"Oh, no! No!" The cry was sudden, low, and heartfelt.

Wimpole squeezed the cold railing a little harder in his hands, but did not move.

"Is there any proof at all that I could give you? Try and think."

"Why should I need proof?" asked Helen. "I believe you, as I always have."

"Well, then—" he began, but she interrupted him.

"That does not change matters," she continued. "You are right merely because you are perfectly disinterested for yourself, and altogether interested for me alone. I am not the only person to be considered."

"I think you are. And if any one else has any right to consideration, it is Archie."

"I know," Helen answered, "and you hurt me again when you say it. But besides all of us, there is Henry."

"And what right has he?" asked Wimpole, almost fiercely. "What right has he to any sort of consideration from you, or from any one? If you had a brother, he would have wrung Harmon's neck long ago! I wish I had the right!"

"I never heard you say anything brutal before," said Helen.

"I never had such good cause," retorted Wimpole, a little more quietly. "Put yourself in my position. I have loved you all my life, — God knows I have loved you honestly, too, — and held my tongue. And Harmon has spent his life in ruining yours in every way, — in ways I know and in ways I don't know, but can more than half guess. He neglected you, he was unfaithful to you, he insulted you, and at last he struck you. I have found that out to-day, and that blow must have nearly killed you. I know about those things. Do you expect me to have any consideration for the brute who has half killed the woman I love? Do you expect me to keep my hands off the man whose hands have struck you and wounded you? By the Lord, Helen, you are expecting too much of human nature! Or too little — I don't know which!"

He had controlled his temper long, keeping down the white heat of it in his heart, but he could not be calm forever. The fighting instinct was not lost yet, and must have its way.

"He did not know what he was doing," said Helen, shrinking a little.

"You have a right to say that," answered the colonel, "if you can be forgiving enough. But only a coward could say it for you, and only a coward would stand by and see you go back to your husband. I am not a coward, and I won't. Since you have cabled to him, I shall leave to night, whether you send that letter or not. Can't you understand?"

"But what can you do? What can you say to him? How can you influence him? Even if I admit that I have no power to keep you from going to him, what can you do when you see him?"

"I can think of that on the way," said Wimpole. "There will be more than enough time. I don't know what I shall say or do yet. It does not matter, for I have made up my mind."

"Will nothing induce you to stay here?" asked Helen, desperately.

"Nothing," answered Wimpole, and his lips shut upon the word.

"Then I will go, too," answered Helen.

"You!" Wimpole had not thought of such a possibility, and he started.

"Yes. My mind is made up, too. If you go, I go. I shall get there as soon as you, and I will prevent you from seeing him at all. If you force me to it, I will defend him from you. I will tell the doctors that you will drive him mad again, and they will help me to protect him. You cannot get there before me, you know, for we shall cross in the same steamer, and land at the same moment."

"What a woman you are!" Wimpole bent his head, as he spoke the words, leaning against the railing. "But I might have known it," he added; "I might have known you would do that. It is like you."

Helen felt a bitter sort of triumph over herself, in having destroyed the last chance of his interference.

"In any case," she said, "I should go at once. It could be a matter of only a few days at the utmost. Why should I wait, since I have made up my mind?"

"Why indeed?" The colonel's voice was sad. "I suppose the martyrs were glad when the waiting was over, and their turn came to be torn to pieces."

He felt that he was annihilated, and he suffered keenly in his defeat, for he had been determined to save her at all risks. She was making even risk impossible. If she went straight to her husband and took him back, and protected him, as she called it, what could any one do? It was a hopeless case. Wimpole's anger against Harmon slowly subsided, and above it rose his pity for the woman who was giving all the life she still had left for the sake of her marriage vow, who was ready, and almost eager, to go back to a state full of horror in the past, and of danger in the future, because she had once solemnly promised to be Henry Harmon's wife, and could not find in all the cruel years a reason for taking back her word. He bowed his head, and he knew that there was something higher in her than he had ever dreamt in his own honourable life, for it was something that clung to its belief, against all suggestion or claim of justice for itself.

It was not only pity. A despair for her crept nearer and grew upon him every moment. Though he had seen her rarely, he had felt nearer to her since Harmon had been mad, and now he was to be further from her than ever before. He would probably not go so far as she feared, and would be willing to enter her husband's house for her sake, and in the hope of being useful to her. But he could never be so near to her again as he was now, and his last chance of protecting her had vanished before her unchangeable resolution. He would almost rather have known that she was going to her death, than see her return to Harmon. He made one more attempt to influence her. He did it roughly, but his voice shook a little.

"It seems to me," he said, "that if I were a woman, I should be too proud to go back to a man who had struck me."

Helen moved and stood upright, trying to look into his face clearly in the dimness as she spoke.

"Then you think I am not proud?"

He could see her white features and dark eyes, and he guessed her expression.

"You are not proud for yourself," he answered rather stubbornly. "If you were, you could not do this."

She turned from him again, and looked down at the black water.

"I am prouder than you think," she said. "That does not make it easier."

"In one way, yes. When you have determined to do a thing, you are ashamed to change your mind, no matter what your decision may cost yourself and others."

"Yes, when I am right. At least, I hope I should be ashamed to break down now."

"I wish you would!"

It was a helpless exclamation, and Wimpole knew it, for he was at the end of all argument and hope, and his despair for her rose in his eyes in the dark. He could neither do nor say anything more, and presently when he had left her at the door of her hotel, she would do what she meant to do, to the letter. For the second time on that day he wished that he had acted, instead of speaking, and that he had set out on his journey without warning her. But in the first place he had believed that she would take more time to consider her action; and again, he had a vague sense that it would not have been loyal and fair to oppose her intention without warning her. And now she had utterly defeated him, and upheld her will against him, in spite of all he could do. He loved her the better for her strength, but he despaired the more. He felt that he was going to say good-bye to her, as though she were about to die.

He put out his hand to take hers, and she met it readily. In her haste to come out with her letter she had not even taken the time to put on gloves, and her warm, firm fingers closed upon his thin hand as though they were the stronger.

"I must go," she said. "It is very late."

"Is it?"

"Yes. I want to thank you, for wishing to

help me — and for everything. I know that you would do anything for me, and I like to feel that you would. But there is nothing to be done. Henry will answer my cable, and then I shall go to him."

"It is as though you were dying, and I were saying good-bye to you, Helen."

"That would be easier," she answered, "for you and me."

She pressed his hand with a frank, unaffected pressure, and then withdrew her own. He sighed as he turned from the dark water to cross the quiet street with her. The people who had been walking about had gone home suddenly, as they do in provincial places, and the electric light glared and blinked upon the deserted, macadamized road. There was something unwontedly desolate, even the air, for the sky was cloudy, and a damp wind came up from the lake.

Without a word the two walked to the post office, and as Wimpole saw the irrevocable message dropped into the slit, his heart almost stopped beating. A faint smile that was cruelly sad to see crossed Helen's white face; a reflexion of the bitter victory she had won over herself against such great odds.

CHAPTER XII

THE two walked slowly and silently along the pavement to the hotel, the damp wind following them in fitful gusts and chilling them as they went. They had no words, for they had said all to each other; each knew that the other was suffering, and both knew that their lives had led them into a path of sadness from which they could not turn back. They walked wearily and unwillingly, side by side, and the way seemed long, and yet too short, as it shortened before them.

At the lighted porch of the hotel they paused, reluctant to part.

"May I see you to-morrow?" asked Wimpole, in a dull voice.

"Yes, I must see you before I go," Helen answered.

In the light of the lamps he saw how pale she was, and how very tired, and she looked at him and knew from his face how he was suffering for her. They joined hands and forgot to part them when their eyes had met. But they had nothing to say, and they had only to bid each other a good night which meant good-bye to both, though they should meet ever so often again.

The porter of the hotel stood in the doorway a few steps above them and watched them with a sort of stolid interest. The lamplight gleamed upon his gilt buttons, and the reflexion of them made Helen aware of his presence. Then he went into the entrance, and there was nobody else about. Voices came with broken laughter from the small garden adjacent to the hotel, where there was a café, and far away, at the end of the entrance hall, the clerk pored over his books.

Still Wimpole held Helen's hand.

"It is very hard," he said.

"It is harder than you know," she answered.

For she loved him, though he did not know it, and she felt as well as he did that she was losing him. But because she was Harmon's wife and meant to stand by her husband, she would not call it love in her heart, though she knew her own secret. She would hardly let herself think that it was much harder for her than for Wimpole, though she knew it. Temptation is not sin. She had killed her temptations that day, and in their death had almost killed herself.

The sacrifice was perfect and whole-hearted, brave as true faith, and final as death itself.

"Good night," said Wimpole, and his voice broke.

Helen still had strength to speak.

"Neither you nor I shall ever regret this," she answered, but she looked long at him, as though she were not to see him again.

He pressed her hand hard and dropped it. Once more she looked at him and then turned slowly and left him standing there.

The porter of the hotel was facing her on the steps. Neither she nor Wimpole had noticed that he had come back and was waiting for them to part. He held a telegram in his hand, and Helen started slightly as she saw it, for she knew that it must be Harmon's answer to her word of forgiveness.

"Already!" she exclaimed faintly, as she took it.

She turned back to Wimpole, and met his eyes again, for he had not moved.

"It is Henry's answer," she said.

She opened the envelope, standing with her back to the light and to the porter. Wimpole breathed hard, and watched her face, and knew that nothing was to be spared to either of them on that day. As she read the words, he thought she swayed a little on her feet, and her eyes opened very wide, and her lips were white. Wimpole watched them and saw how strangely they moved, as if she were trying to speak and could not. He set his teeth, for he believed that even the short message had in it some fresh insult or injury for her.

She reeled visibly, and steadied herself against one of the pillars of the porch, but she was able to hold out the thin scrap of paper to Wimpole as he moved forwards to catch her. He read it. It was a cable notice through the telegraph office from Brest.

"Your message number 731 Henry Harmon New York not delivered owing to death of the person addressed."

Wimpole read the words twice before their meaning stunned him. When he knew where he was, his eyes were still on the paper, and he was grasping Helen's wrist, while she stood stark and straight against the pillar of the porch. She lifted her free hand and passed it slowly across her forehead, opening and shutting her eyes as if waking. The porter stared at her from the steps.

"Come," said Wimpole. "Let us go out again. We can't stay here."

Helen looked at him, only half comprehending. Even in the uncertain light he could see the colour returning to her face, and he felt it in his own. Then her senses came back all at once with her own clear judgment and decision, and the longing to be alone, which he could not understand, as he tried to draw her away with him.

"No, no!" she cried, resisting. "Let me go, please let me go! Please!"

He had already dropped her wrist.

"Come to-morrow," she added quickly.

And all her lost youth was in her as she lightly turned and went from him up the steps. Again he stood still, following her with his eyes, but an age had passed, with Harmon's life, between that time and this.

He understood better, when he himself was alone, walking far on, through the damp wind, by the shore of the lake, past the big railway station, just then in one of its fits of silence, past the wooden piers built out into the lake for the steamers, and out beyond, not counting his steps, nor seeing things, with bent head, and one hand catching nervously at the breast of his coat.

He understood Helen, for he also had need of being alone to face the tremendous contrast of the hour and to digest in secret the huge joy he was ashamed to show to himself, because it was for the death of a man whose existence had darkened his own. Because Harmon was suddenly dead, the sleeping hope of twenty years had waked with deep life and strength. Time and age were rolled away like a mist before the morning breeze, the world was young again, and the rose of yesterday was once more the lovely flower of to-day.

Yet he was too brave a man, and too good, to let himself rejoice cruelly in Harmon's death, any more than he would have gloried, in his younger days, over an enemy fallen in fight. But it was hard to struggle against this instinct, deep rooted and strong in humanity ages before Achilles dragged Hector round the walls of Troy. Christianity has made it mean to insult the dead and their memory. For what we call honour comes to us from chivalry and knighthood, which grew out of Christian doings when men believed; and though non-Christian people have their standards of right and wrong, they have not our sort of honour, nor anything like it, and cannot in the least understand it.

But Wimpole was made happy by Harmon's death, and he himself could not deny it. That was another matter, and one over which he had no control. His satisfaction was in the main disinterested, being on Helen's behalf; for though he hoped, he was very far from believing that she would marry him, now that she was a widow. He had not even guessed that she had loved him long. It was chiefly because his whole nature had been suffering so sincerely for her sake during the long hours since he had read the paragraph in the paper, that he was now so immensely happy. He tried to call up again the last conversation in the dark, by the river; but though the words both he and she had spoken came back in broken echoes, they seemed to have no meaning, and he could not explain to himself how he could possibly have stood there, wrenching at the cold iron rail to steady his nerves, less than half an hour ago. It was incredible. He felt like a man who has been in the delirium of a fever, in which he has talked foolishly and struck out wildly at his friends, and who cannot believe such things of himself when he is recovering, though he dimly remembers them, with a sort of half-amused shame for his weakness.

Wimpole did not know how long he wandered by the lake in the windy darkness, before he felt that he had control of speech and action again and found himself near the bridge, going towards his hotel. It was less than half an hour, perhaps, but ever afterwards, when he thought of it, he seemed to have walked up and down all night, a hundred times past the railway station, a hundred times along the row of steamboat piers, struggling with the impression that he had no right to be perfectly happy, and fighting off the instinct to rejoice in Harmon's death.

But Helen had fled to her own room and had locked the door upon the world. To her, as to Wimpole, it would have seemed horrible to be frankly glad that her husband was dead. But she had no such instinct. She had been dazed beyond common sense and speech by the sudden relief from the strain she had borne so strongly and bravely. She had been dazzled by the light of freedom as a man let out of a dark prison after half a lifetime of captivity. She had been half stunned by the instant release of all the springs of her nature, long forced back upon themselves by the sheer strength of her conscience. And yet she was sorry for the dead man.

Far away in her past youth she remembered his handsome face, his bright eyes, his strong vitality, his pleasant voice, and the low ringing tone of it that had touched her and brought her to the ruin of her marriage, and she remembered that for a time she had half loved him and believed love whole. She is a hard and cruel woman who has not a little pitiful tenderness left for a dead past,—though it be buried under a hideous present,—and some kind memory of the man she has called dear.

Helen thought of his face as he was lying

dead now, white and stony, but somehow, in her kindness, it became the face of long ago, and was not like him as when she had seen him last. The touch of death is strangely healing. She had no tears, but there was a dim softness in her eyes, for the man who was gone; not for the man who had insulted her, tortured her, struck her, but for the husband she had married long ago.

The other, the incarnate horror of her mature life, had dropped from existence, leaving his place full of the light in which she was thereafter to live, and in the bright peace she saw Wimpole's face, as he waited for her.

In the midst of her thoughts was the enigmatic spectre of the world, the familiar tormentor of those with whom the world has anything to do — a vast, disquieting question-mark to their actions. What would the world say, when she married Wimpole?

What could it say? It knew, if it knew anything of her, that her husband had been little better than a beast — no better; worse, perhaps. It knew that Wimpole was a man in thousands, and perhaps it knew that he had been faithful to her mere name in his heart during the best of his years. She had no enemies to cast a shadow upon her future by slurring her past.

Yet she had heard the world talk, and the names of women who had married old friends within the first year of widowhood were rarely untouched by scandal. She did not fear that, but in her heart there was a sort of unacknowledged dread lest Wimpole, who was growing old in patience, should be patient to the end out of some over-fine scruple for her fair name.

Then came the thought of her new widowhood and rebuked her, and with the old habit of fighting battles against her heart for her conscience, she turned fiercely against her long-silent love that was crying freedom so loudly in her ears. Harmon just dead, not buried yet, perhaps, and she already thinking of marriage! Said in those words, it seemed contemptible, though all her loyalty to her husband had been for a word's sake, almost since the beginning.

But then, again, as she closed her eyes to think sensibly, she set her lips to stay the smile at her scruples. Her loyalty had been all for the vow, for the meaning of the bond, for the holiness of marriage itself. It had not been the loyalty of love for Harmon, and Harmon being dead, its only object was gone. The rest, the mourning for the unloved dead, was a canon of the world, not a law of God. For decency, she would wear black for a short time, but in her heart she was free, and free in her conscience.

To the last, she had borne all, and had been ready to bear more. Her last word had gone at once, with the message of forgiveness he had asked, and though he had been dead before it reached him he could not have doubted her answer, for he knew her. If she had been near him, she would have been with him to the end, to help him, and to comfort him if she could. She had been ready to go back to him, and the letter that was to have told him so was already gone upon its fruitless journey, to return to her after a long time as a reminder of what she had been willing to bear. She could not reproach herself with any weakness or omission, and her reason told her plainly that although she must mourn outwardly to please the world, it would be folly to refuse her heart the thought of a happiness for which she had paid beforehand with half a lifetime of pain.

When that was all at once and unmistakably clear to her, she let her head sink gently back upon the cushion of the chair, her set lips parted, and she softly sighed, as though the day were done at last and her rest had come. As she sat there, the lines of sorrow and suffering were smoothed away and the faint colour crept slowly and naturally to her cheeks, as her eyes closed by slow degrees under the shaded light of the lamp. One more restful sigh, her sweet breath came slower and more evenly, one hand fell upon her knee with upward palm and loosened fingers that did not move again; she was asleep.

CHAPTER XIII

So ends the history of a day unforgotten in the memories of the men and women, young and old, for whom it chanced to be life's turning-point. Looking back into the full, past years through which the fight has been fought, most of us still know one day and hour in which the tide of battle turned; we see the faces that rose up against us, and those that stood beside us in the struggle; we hear the words spoken which cheered us to the great charge, or turned our hearts cold and our daring to fear; even our bodily hearts, handfuls of wandering atoms of which not one is left in us from those times, answer the deep memory and beat loud, or fail, as those other atoms did in the decisive instant when one blow more meant victory, and one blow less, defeat.

Helen's last letter to her husband came back to her like a ghost, after many weeks, when she was going over Harmon's papers. There it lay, unopened, as she had sealed it, full of the words that had seemed to cost her life — the promise to pay a debt not justly owed, which no man could claim now. She burned it unread, for she knew every line of it by heart. To read it, even to glance at the writing, she thought, would rouse some pride in her for what she had done and stir a sort of gladness in her soul, because the man was dead and she was safe from him forever. She would not let herself feel such things. Unconsciously she had fought with herself for a principle, not, as most of us do, for the intimate satisfaction of having done right, which is in itself a reward, an object, and an aim for ambition, and therefore not wholly unselfish, not wholly noble, though often both high and worthy.

Right, as we understand it, is the law for each individual, the principle is for all mankind; and as the whole is greater than any of its parts, so is the principle greater than the law. The law says, "Whosoever sheddeth man's blood, by man shall his blood be shed." But the Blood which was shed for all men required of man no lawful avenging.

Moreover, law and all forms of law are only deductions made by the intelligence from the right instincts of the people's heart. Laws which are evolved out of existing circumstances, backwards, as it were, to correct bad results, are rarely anything more than measures of expediency and have not much lasting power. They are medicines, not nourishment for humanity — a cure for the sick, not a rule of life for the sound and whole.

When such enactments of law-givers tend against those impulses which spring from the roots of human feeling, taking into consideration the happiness of the few and not the good of the many, they are bad medicines for the world. The instant, quick release by divorce from all troubles, great and small, between man and wife, is no better than that other instant, quick relief from bodily pain, which is morphia, a material danger no longer at all dim or shadowy.

We are a cowardly generation, and men shrink from suffering now, as their fathers shrank from dishonour in rougher times. The Lotus hangs within the reach of all, and in the lives of many " it is always afternoon," as for the Lotus Eaters. The fruit takes many shapes and names; it is called Divorce, it is called Morphia, it is called Compromise, it is designated in a thousand ways and justified by ten thousand specious arguments, but it means only one thing: Escape from Pain.

Soft-hearted and weak-nerved people ask why humanity should suffer at all, and they hail every invention, moral or material, which can make life easier for the moment, as a heaven-sent blessing. Why should we be uncomfortable, even an hour, when a little dose of poison can create a lazy oblivion? That is the drunkard's reasoning, the opium-eater's defence, the invalid's excuse. It is no argument for men who call themselves the world's masters.

Civilization and Progress are not the same thing. We have too much progress and too little civilization nowadays. Progress is omnivorous, eager after new things, seeking above all to save trouble and get money. Civilization is eclectic, slow, painstaking, wise, willing to buy good at the price it is worth. Civilization gave us marriage, in respecting which we are above animals. Progress is giving us divorce, wholesale, cheap, immoral, a degradation beneath that of those primitive peoples, who make no promises and break none, who do not set up right as a fashion and wrong as a practice, the truth for the ensign and the lie for the course.

Helen Harmon's existence turned out happily in the end. She was fortunate at last, before the love of life was gone. But for the accident of her husband's sudden death, she would have had to face her cruel difficulties to death's solution; and with her character she would not have been defeated, for she had on her side the accumulated force of all womanliness against the individual evil that was her familiar enemy.

Far should it be from the story-teller to draw a moral; furthest of all, that false moral that makes faith and truth and courage get worldly pay for their services — servants to be hired as guides and porters to happiness. In Helen's case it chanced that she got what she wanted. Fate had spent its force against her, and peace was with her thereafter.

Even "poor Archie" found his vocation at last. The day that had meant so much to many had brought him a sort of awakening of mind, an increase of reason and a growth of character. His one strong instinct became a dominating force. He would save life, many lives, so long as he had strength. Sylvia would never care for him, of course; he said to himself that she should at least see what he could do. He remembered with constant longing the wild delight he had felt when he had brought the little child safely to the deck of the ferryboat on the North River, and when, bruised and bleeding, he had stopped the bolting horses in the New York street.

He unfolded his plan to the colonel first, because he was a man, and must understand; then he told his mother. There was nothing to be said against it, except that it was dangerous. He had made up his mind to join a Life-Saving Station on the coast. It was the one thing he could do, and he knew it.

"Of course," he said, with his elementary philosophy, "if I get drowned the first time, there won't be anything gained. But if I can help to save a few people before that, it won't matter so much, you know. It'll be like money, when you get something for it."

The rude bravery of the argument brought a look into Wimpole's eyes which had not been there for a long time. Helen had a lump in her throat.

"But if anything should happen to you —" she began, and stopped.

"Well, then," answered Archie, "I suppose I'd go to heaven, shouldn't I? And that would be all right, just the same."

And thereupon he began to whistle thoughtfully. It was very simple in his eyes, and very desirable. Life seemed to him to be man's first and greatest possession, as it is. For him, its possibilities were small, but he had a dim perception of its value to others, whom he called "clever" in wholesale distinction from himself. It was worth having, worth keeping, and worth saving, for them, at the risk of his own.

As for Miss Rachel Wimpole, as soon as she heard of Harmon's death, she knew that her brother would marry Helen. She had systematically disapproved of his life-long devotion to a woman beyond his reach, while she had involuntarily respected in him the same unchanging faithfulness which had guarded her own heart against everything else for so many years, a little stronghold of no great importance to the rest of the world, but which held all that was most dear and precious to her. So here and there, in the chaos of the middle ages, some strong, poor gentleman, a mere atom in the wide Holy Empire, may have kept his small castle and his narrow acres of meagre land against all comers.

When Harmon was dead and gone, Miss Wimpole's disapprobation instantly disappeared, and she never at any time afterwards seemed to remember how she had felt about the matter during so many years. Wimpole approached her with some diffidence, and she met him with genuine enthusiasm. She was one of those rare people who can make others vicars of their happiness, so to say, whose place has been long darkened by sad clouds, but who see the sunshine far away on another's land and are glad for that other one's sake.

It is a sign of our times that a man whose fancy leads him now and then to make a story of characters almost ideal, should feel as if he owed his reader a sort of apology for so far disregarding the common fashion. There must always be a conflict between the real and the ideal, between what we are told is knowledge and what our hearts tell us is truth, between the evil men do and the good which is beyond their strength, but not above their aspiration. And therefore the old question stands unanswered: Do most people wish to be shown what they are, or what they might be? In order to avoid the difficulty of replying, fashion comes forward and says to-day that art is truth, and infers that art must be accurate and photographic and closely imitative.

What has art to do with truth? Is not truth the imagination's deadly enemy? If the two meet, they must fight to the death. It is therefore better, in principle, to keep them apart, and let each survive separately with their uses. Two and two make four, says Truth. Never mind facts, says Art, let us imagine a world in which two and two make five, and see whether we can get anything pleasant, or amusing, out of the supposition. Let us sometimes talk about men and women who are unimaginably perfect, and let us find out what they would do with the troubles that make sinners of most of us, and puzzle us, and turn our hair grey.

Matter, says the mystic, is the inexhaustible source and active cause of all harm. Imagination can be altogether free from matter. That is what we mean by the ideal, and men may say what they will, it is worth having. A man must know the enemy against whom he is matched, if he hopes to win; he must know his adversary's fence, his thrusts and feints and parries. Truth will give him that knowledge. But beyond the enemy, and beyond victory over him, there is the aspiration, the hope, the aim of all life — and that is the ideal, if it is anything at all worth hoping; it is transcendent, outside of all facts and perhaps of any attainment, and only the imagination can ever tell us what it may be.

Yet those who guess at it, dwell on it and love it, and it comes to be the better part of their lives. The world holds two great classes of mankind, artists and truth-seekers. There are millions of artists, there always have been, and there always will be. One in each million, perhaps, is born with the gift of creation and knows the tools of his trade by instinct, and works with them, as soon as he is old enough to think. The rest are not less artists, because they are not producers. They have the same aspirations, the same longings, the same tastes, though they are not makers, as he is; and when he has finished his work, they look at it with eyes like his, and enjoy even more perfectly than he, for they see the expression of a thought like their own, while all that he could not express is hidden from them and does not disturb their satisfaction. Art for art's sake, if such a thing could be, would mean that the one man would work just as hard to give his imagination a shape, even if the rest of the million were not there to understand him. But he knows that they are all living and that the ideal for which he labours is divine to them all, whether he fail or whether he succeed.

THE END

TAQUISARA.

BY

F. MARION CRAWFORD,

Author of "Saracinesca," "Pietro Ghisleri," "Katharine Lauderdale," "The Ralstons," etc.

Two Volumes. 16mo. In Box, $2.00.

"Mr. Crawford once more shows that mastery of his art which entitles him to rank among the very foremost of living novelists. . . . The interest of the reader is at once compelled, while there is enacted a drama as dark and terrible as some legend of the Medici or the Borgias, and so exquisite is the art of the narrator that the reader's interest is never suffered to relax.

"'Taquisara' the Sicilian, the Princess Veronica, and the invalid Gianluca are characters drawn with the power and poetic feeling that Mr. Crawford's readers know so well." — *New York Sun.*

"The plot needs no telling; it is one of Mr. Crawford's best, and the scene, Naples, and the mountain country back of it, united with the characteristics and temperaments of the Italian people, give the noted author splendid opportunities to realize his best work. Mr. Crawford continues to reap fame with every novel that comes from his pen." — *Boston Budget.*

"'Taquisara' in vigor of language and sustained interest of plot easily ranks with Mr. Crawford's best work, which, by the way, is quite as good as the best by any living writer." — *Oneonta Herald.*

"'Taquisara,' as its name indicates, is another of Mr. Crawford's happily told stories of Italian life, and must find many admirers. Here the author is at his best. He knows his Italy — who could have read his 'Casa Braccio' and not been conscious of it? In this last novel the interest is unflagging, and all the imaginative charm and literary force which belong to the author are to be found."

THE MACMILLAN COMPANY,

66 FIFTH AVENUE, NEW YORK.

CASA BRACCIO.

BY

F. MARION CRAWFORD.

WITH THIRTEEN FULL-PAGE ILLUSTRATIONS FROM DRAWINGS
BY CASTAIGNE.

Buckram. 2 vols., in box. $2.00.

PRESS COMMENTS.

" Mr. Crawford's latest novel, 'Casa Braccio,' may not improbably come to be regarded as the supreme masterpiece in fiction — of the English tongue at least — that has appeared since 'Daniel Deronda.' Its breadth of human emotion, its vividness of individualities, its splendor of coloring, all entitle this novel to a lasting place in the literature of fiction." — *Chicago Inter-Ocean*.

" Mr. Crawford has won success in two different fields of fiction. In this, his present work, he combines these fields, and wins a greater success than ever. There is but little question that 'Casa Braccio' will prove to be the great novel of the year." — *Boston Daily Advertiser*.

"We are grateful when Mr. Crawford keeps to his Italy. The poetry and enchantment of the land are all his own, and 'Casa Braccio' gives promise of being his masterpiece. . . . He has the life, the beauty, the heart and the soul of Italy at the tips of his fingers." — *Los Angeles Express*.

" Admirably strong and impressive." — *Boston Beacon*.

" From all points of view 'Casa Braccio' is the most artistically finished, dramatic, and powerful work Mr. Crawford has produced." — *New York World*.

"The people who are fond of prating about the thinness of American novels should read 'Casa Braccio,' for it is rich in all the qualities that go to make up a good story. . . . It is safe to say that any one who reads one or two of Crawford's stories will extend his acquaintance with this singularly versatile and charming writer." — *San Francisco Chronicle*.

THE MACMILLAN COMPANY,
66 FIFTH AVENUE, NEW YORK.

THE RALSTONS.

A Sequel to "Katharine Lauderdale."

BY

F. MARION CRAWFORD.

2 vols. 16mo. Cloth. $2.00.

PRESS COMMENTS.

"The interest is unflagging throughout. Never has the author done more brilliant, artistic work than here." — *Ohio State Journal.*

"It is immensely entertaining; once in the full swing of the narrative, one is carried on quite irresistibly to the end. The style throughout is easy and graceful, and the text abounds in wise and witty reflections on the realities of existence." — *Boston Beacon.*

"The book is admirably written; it contains passages full of distinction; it is instinct with intensity of purpose; the characters are drawn with a living touch." — *London Daily News.*

"Mr. Crawford's new story, 'The Ralstons,' is as powerful a work as any that has come from his pen.... Harmonized by a strength and warmth of imagination uncommon in modern fiction, the story will be heartily enjoyed by every one who reads it." — *Edinburgh Scotsman.*

"As a picture of a certain kind of New York life, it is correct and literal; as a study of human nature, it is realistic enough to be modern, and romantic enough to be of the age of Trollope."—*Chicago Herald.*

"The whole group of character studies is strong and vivid." — *Literary World.*

"Mr. Crawford's pen portraits are wonderfully vivid. His analysis of motive is keen and subtle. His portrayal of passion, be it love or avarice, is most graphic." — *Boston Advertiser.*

THE MACMILLAN COMPANY,
66 FIFTH AVENUE, NEW YORK.

UNIFORM EDITION

OF THE WORKS OF

F. MARION CRAWFORD.

12mo. Cloth. Price $1.00 per volume.

KATHARINE LAUDERDALE.

The first of a series of novels dealing with New York life.

"Mr. Crawford at his best is a great novelist, and in 'Katharine Lauderdale' we have him at his best." — *Boston Daily Advertiser.*

"A most admirable novel, excellent in style, flashing with humor, and full of the ripest and wisest reflections upon men and women." — *The Westminster Gazette.*

"It is the first time, we think, in American fiction that any such breadth of view has shown itself in the study of our social framework." — *Life.*

"It need scarcely be said that the story is skilfully and picturesquely written, portraying sharply individual characters in well-defined surroundings." — *New York Commercial Advertiser.*

"'Katharine Lauderdale' is a tale of New York, and is up to the highest level of his work. In some respects it will probably be regarded as his best. None of his works, with the exception of 'Mr. Isaacs,' shows so clearly his skill as a literary artist." — *San Francisco Evening Bulletin.*

PIETRO GHISLERI.

"The imaginative richness, the marvellous ingenuity of plot, the power and subtlety of the portrayal of character, the charm of the romantic environment, — the entire atmosphere, indeed, — rank this novel at once among the great creations." — *The Boston Budget.*

THE MACMILLAN COMPANY,
66 FIFTH AVENUE, NEW YORK.

SARACINESCA.

"His highest achievement, as yet, in the realms of fiction. The work has two distinct merits, either of which would serve to make it great, — that of telling a perfect story in a perfect way, and of giving a graphic picture of Roman society in the last days of the pope's temporal power. . . . The story is exquisitely told." — *Boston Traveler.*

"One of the most engrossing novels we have ever read." — *Boston Times.*

SANT' ILARIO.

A sequel to "Saracinesca."

"The author shows steady and constant improvement in his art. 'Sant' Ilario' is a continuation of the chronicles of the Saracinesca family. . . . A singularly powerful and beautiful story. . . . Admirably developed, with a naturalness beyond praise. . . . It must rank with 'Greifenstein' as the best work the author has produced. It fulfils every requirement of artistic fiction. It brings out what is most impressive in human action, without owing any of its effectiveness to sensationalism or artifice. It is natural, fluent in evolution, accordant with experience, graphic in description, penetrating in analysis, and absorbing in interest." — *New York Tribune.*

DON ORSINO.

A continuation of "Saracinesca" and "Sant' Ilario."

"The third in a rather remarkable series of novels dealing with three generations of the Saracinesca family, entitled respectively 'Saracinesca,' 'Sant' Ilario,' and 'Don Orsino,' and these novels present an important study of Italian life, customs, and conditions during the present century. Each one of these novels is worthy of very careful reading, and offers exceptional enjoyment in many ways, in the fascinating absorption of good fiction, in interest of faithful historic accuracy, and in charm of style. The 'new Italy' is strikingly revealed in 'Don Orsino.'" — *Boston Budget.*

"We are inclined to regard the book as the most ingenious of all Mr. Crawford's fictions. Certainly it is the best novel of the season." — *Evening Bulletin.*

THE MACMILLAN COMPANY,
66 FIFTH AVENUE, NEW YORK.

WITH THE IMMORTALS.

"Altogether an admirable piece of art worked in the spirit of a thorough artist. Every reader of cultivated tastes will find it a book prolific in entertainment of the most refined description, and to all such we commend it heartily." — *Boston Saturday Evening Gazette.*

"The strange central idea of the story could have occurred only to a writer whose mind was very sensitive to the current modern thought and progress, while its execution, the setting it forth in proper literary clothing, could be successfully attempted only by one whose active literary ability should be fully equalled by his power of assimilative knowledge both literary and scientific, and no less by his courage and capacity for hard work. The book will be found to have a fascination entirely new for the habitual reader of novels. Indeed, Mr. Crawford has succeeded in taking his readers quite above the ordinary plane of novel interest." — *Boston Advertiser.*

MARZIO'S CRUCIFIX.

"We take the liberty of saying that this work belongs to the highest department of character-painting in words." — *Churchman.*

"We have repeatedly had occasion to say that Mr. Crawford possesses in an extraordinary degree the art of constructing a story. His sense of proportion is just, and his narrative flows along with ease and perspicuity. It is as if it could not have been written otherwise, so naturally does the story unfold itself, and so logical and consistent is the sequence of incident after incident. As a story 'Marzio's Crucifix' is perfectly constructed." — *New York Commercial Advertiser.*

KHALED.

A Story of Arabia.

"Throughout the fascinating story runs the subtlest analysis, suggested rather than elaborately worked out, of human passion and motive, the building out and development of the character of the woman who becomes the hero's wife and whose love he finally wins, being an especially acute and highly finished example of the story-teller's art. . . . That it is beautifully written and holds the interest of the reader, fanciful as it all is, to the very end, none who know the depth and artistic finish of Mr. Crawford's work need be told." — *The Chicago Times.*

PAUL PATOFF.

THE MACMILLAN COMPANY,
66 FIFTH AVENUE, NEW YORK.

MR. ISAACS.
A Tale of Modern India.

"The writer first shows the hero in relation with the people of the East and then skilfully brings into connection the Anglo-Saxon race. It is in this showing of the different effects which the two classes of minds have upon the central figure of the story that one of its chief merits lies. The characters are original, and one does not recognize any of the hackneyed personages who are so apt to be considered indispensable to novelists, and which, dressed in one guise or another, are but the marionettes, which are all dominated by the same mind, moved by the same motive force. The men are all endowed with individualism and independent life and thought. . . . There is a strong tinge of mysticism about the book which is one of its greatest charms." — *Boston Transcript.*

"No story of human experience that we have met with since 'John Inglesant' has such an effect of transporting the reader into regions differing from his own. 'Mr. Isaacs' is the best novel that has ever laid its scenes in our Indian dominions." — *The Daily News, London.*

DR. CLAUDIUS.
A True Story.

"There is a suggestion of strength, of a mastery of facts, of a fund of knowledge, that speaks well for future production. . . . To be thoroughly enjoyed, however, this book must be read, as no mere cursory notice can give an adequate idea of its many interesting points and excellences, for without a doubt 'Dr. Claudius' is the most interesting book that has been published for many months, and richly deserves a high place in the public favor." — *St. Louis Spectator.*

"To our mind it by no means belies the promises of its predecessor. The story, an exceedingly improbable and romantic one, is told with much skill; the characters are strongly marked without any suspicion of caricature, and the author's ideas on social and political subjects are often brilliant and always striking. It is no exaggeration to say that there is not a dull page in the book, which is peculiarly adapted for the recreation of student or thinker." — *Living Church.*

TO LEEWARD.

"A story of remarkable power." — *Review of Reviews.*

"Mr. Crawford has written many strange and powerful stories of Italian life, but none can be any stranger or more powerful than 'To Leeward,' with its mixture of comedy and tragedy, innocence and guilt." — *Cottage Hearth.*

THE MACMILLAN COMPANY,
66 FIFTH AVENUE, NEW YORK.

A CIGARETTE-MAKER'S ROMANCE.

"It is a touching romance, filled with scenes of great dramatic power." — *Boston Commercial Bulletin.*

"It is full of life and movement, and is one of the best of Mr. Crawford's books." — *Boston Saturday Evening Gazette.*

"The interest is unflagging throughout. Never has Mr. Crawford done more brilliant realistic work than here. But his realism is only the case and cover for those intense feelings which, placed under no matter what humble conditions, produce the most dramatic and the most tragic situations. . . . This is a secret of genius, to take the most coarse and common material, the meanest surroundings, the most sordid material prospects, and out of the vehement passions which sometimes dominate all human beings to build up with these poor elements scenes and passages, the dramatic and emotional power of which at once enforce attention and awaken the profoundest interest." — *New York Tribune.*

GREIFENSTEIN.

"'Greifenstein' is a remarkable novel, and while it illustrates once more the author's unusual versatility, it also shows that he has not been tempted into careless writing by the vogue of his earlier books. . . . There is nothing weak or small or frivolous in the story. The author deals with tremendous passions working at the height of their energy. His characters are stern, rugged, determined men and women, governed by powerful prejudices and iron conventions, types of a military people, in whom the sense of duty has been cultivated until it dominates all other motives, and in whom the principle of 'noblesse oblige' is, so far as the aristocratic class is concerned, the fundamental rule of conduct. What such people may be capable of is startlingly shown." — *New York Tribune.*

A ROMAN SINGER.

"One of Mr. Crawford's most charming stories — a love romance pure and simple." — *Boston Home Journal.*

"'A Roman Singer' is one of his most finished, compact, and successful stories, and contains a splendid picture of Italian life." — *Toronto Mail.*

THE MACMILLAN COMPANY,
66 FIFTH AVENUE, NEW YORK.

THE THREE FATES.

"The strength of the story lies in its portrayal of the aspirations, disciplinary efforts, trials, and triumphs of the man who is a born writer, and who, by long and painful experiences, learns the good that is in him and the way in which to give it effectual expression. The analytical quality of the book is excellent, and the individuality of each one of the very dissimilar three fates is set forth in an entirely satisfactory manner. . . . Mr. Crawford has manifestly brought his best qualities as a student of human nature and his finest resources as a master of an original and picturesque style to bear upon this story. Taken for all in all it is one of the most pleasing of all his productions in fiction, and it affords a view of certain phases of American, or perhaps we should say of New York, life that have not hitherto been treated with anything like the same adequacy and felicity." — *Boston Beacon.*

CHILDREN OF THE KING.

A Tale of Southern Italy.

"A sympathetic reader cannot fail to be impressed with the dramatic power of this story. The simplicity of nature, the uncorrupted truth of a soul, have been portrayed by a master-hand. The suddenness of the unforeseen tragedy at the last renders the incident of the story powerful beyond description. One can only feel such sensations as the last scene of the story incites. It may be added that if Mr. Crawford has written some stories unevenly, he has made no mistakes in the stories of Italian life. A reader of them cannot fail to gain a clearer, fuller acquaintance with the Italians and the artistic spirit that pervades the country." — M. L. B. in *Syracuse Journal.*

THE WITCH OF PRAGUE.

A Fantastic Tale.

ILLUSTRATED BY W. J. HENNESSY.

"'The Witch of Prague' is so remarkable a book as to be certain of as wide a popularity as any of its predecessors. The keenest interest for most readers will lie in its demonstration of the latest revelations of hypnotic science. . . . It is a romance of singular daring and power." — *London Academy.*

"Mr. Crawford has written in many keys, but never in so strange a one as that which dominates 'The Witch of Prague.' . . . The artistic skill with which this extraordinary story is constructed and carried out is admirable and delightful. . . . Mr. Crawford has scored a decided triumph, for the interest of the tale is sustained throughout. . . . A very remarkable, powerful, and interesting story." — *New York Tribune.*

THE MACMILLAN COMPANY,
66 FIFTH AVENUE, NEW YORK.

ZOROASTER.

"The field of Mr. Crawford's imagination appears to be unbounded. . . . In 'Zoroaster' Mr. Crawford's winged fancy ventures a daring flight. . . . Yet 'Zoroaster' is a novel rather than a drama. It is a drama in the force of its situations and in the poetry and dignity of its language; but its men and women are not men and women of a play. By the naturalness of their conversation and behavior they seem to live and lay hold of our human sympathy more than the same characters on a stage could possibly do." — *The Times.*

A TALE OF A LONELY PARISH.

"It is a pleasure to have anything so perfect of its kind as this brief and vivid story. . . . It is doubly a success, being full of human sympathy, as well as thoroughly artistic in its nice balancing of the unusual with the commonplace, the clever juxtaposition of innocence and guilt, comedy and tragedy, simplicity and intrigue." — *Critic.*

"Of all the stories Mr. Crawford has written, it is the most dramatic, the most finished, the most compact. . . . The taste which is left in one's mind after the story is finished is exactly what the fine reader desires and the novelist intends. . . . It has no defects. It is neither trifling nor trivial. It is a work of art. It is perfect." — *Boston Beacon.*

MARION DARCHE.

"Full enough of incident to have furnished material for three or four stories. . . . A most interesting and engrossing book. Every page unfolds new possibilities, and the incidents multiply rapidly." — *Detroit Free Press.*

"We are disposed to rank 'Marion Darche' as the best of Mr. Crawford's American stories." — *The Literary World.*

AN AMERICAN POLITICIAN.

THE NOVEL: What It Is.

18mo. Cloth. 75 Cents.

"When a master of his craft speaks, the public may well listen with careful attention, and since no fiction-writer of the day enjoys in this country a broader or more enlightened popularity than Marion Crawford, his explanation of 'The Novel; What It Is,' will be received with flattering interest." — *The Boston Beacon.*

THE MACMILLAN COMPANY,
66 FIFTH AVENUE, NEW YORK.